CWr
2/8/08

*Understanding and Managing Risk
Attitude*

Managers looking to move to higher levels of risk management maturity in their organisations will find much insight and guidance in this innovative book.
Prof Graham M. Winch, Centre for Research in the Management of Projects,
Manchester Business School

This book provides a pivotal insight into the complexities of human behaviour, psychological influences and subconscious preferences that determine how people initially respond to significant uncertainty ... and creates a road map to change risk attitude if it is both necessary and desirable.
Carl West, Operations Auditor, British Waterways

This book highlights how risk attitude factors influence the human psyche, and carefully explains the impacts. Organisations seeking to dramatically improve the effectiveness of their risk management process will want to use this book's insights.
Craig Peterson, President, PMI Risk Management SIG

This book has prompted me to think more deeply as a change director.
Jon Bassett, Director of Implementation, AXA Life UK

Understanding and Managing Risk Attitude

Second Edition

DAVID HILLSON and
RUTH MURRAY-WEBSTER

GOWER

Published by
Gower Publishing Limited
Gower House
Croft Road
Aldershot
Hants GU11 3HR
England

Gower Publishing Company
Suite 420
101 Cherry Street
Burlington,
VT 05401-4405
USA

David Hillson and Ruth Murray-Webster have asserted their right under the Copyright, Designs and Patents Act 1988 to be identified as the authors of this work.

British Library Cataloguing in Publication Data
Hillson, David, 1955-
   Understanding and managing risk attitude
   1. Risk management
   I. Title II. Murray-Webster, Ruth
   658.1'55

   ISBN 978-0-566-08798-1

Library of Congress Cataloging-in-Publication Data
Hillson, David, 1955–
   Understanding and managing risk attitude / by David Hillson and Ruth Murray-Webster. -- 2nd ed.
     p. cm.
   Includes bibliographical references and index.
   ISBN: 978-0-566-08798-1
   1. Risk management. I. Murray-Webster, Ruth. II. Title.

   HD61.H48 2007
   658.15'5--dc22

                                                                          2006036036

Typeset by IML Typographers, Birkenhead, Merseyside and
Printed in Great Britain by TJ International Ltd, Padstow, Cornwall.

Contents

List of Figures

List of Tables

ATTITUDE

Charles Swindoll
(1934–)

The longer I live, the more I realise the impact of attitude on life. Attitude, to me, is more important than facts. It is more important than the past, than education, than money, than circumstances, than failures, than successes, than what other people think or say or do. It is more important than appearance, giftedness or skills. It will make or break a company or a home. The remarkable thing is we have a choice every day regarding the attitude we will embrace for that day. We cannot change our past. We cannot change the fact that people will act in a certain way. We cannot change the inevitable. The only thing we can do is play on the one string we have, and that is our attitude. I am convinced that life is 10% what happens to me and 90% how I react to it. And so it is with you – we are in charge of our attitudes.

Foreword

We all live in a world full of risk, and on a daily basis we can either choose to take a decision where the outcome is uncertain, or choose not to. Faced with innumerable risks, most people have developed habits and strategies for dealing with the uncertainty in such a way that their lives 'free-flow' most of the time. It is only in the presence of an extraordinary risk that people are usually conscious of the need to make a choice.

The management of these extraordinary, uncertain situations has become a discipline in its own right over the past decades, particularly in a business context, but increasingly also in a social setting. As a result many aspects of risk management are well defined, tried, tested and trusted – though not all. This book addresses one facet of risk management that is not well understood, namely risk attitudes.

Our motivation in writing the first edition in 2005 was to shed light on an area that on the one hand is seen as rational and logical, but on the other involves the deepest workings of the human brain. We aimed to share with our readers our fascination with the human influence on decision-making in risky situations.

Our intention was to provide a book that is informative and thought-provoking, yet practical in nature; feedback suggests that were successful in that regard.

Since publication of the first edition our assumption has been confirmed that many readers want to learn how to understand and manage risk attitudes so that they can apply the learning to risky business situations, for example those associated with safety risk, project and programme risk, financial risk and so on. The feedback we have gained confirms that the book certainly helps in these areas.

Even more importantly though, our hope, then and now, is that business readers will engage with the text at a personal level and learn more about understanding and managing their own risk attitudes in life situations outside the workplace.

We know that those readers who apply what we have written to their professional lives benefit through deliberately understanding and managing their risk attitudes. We also know that those who have reflected on the relevance of the subject to all aspects of their lives and applied the guidance there have benefited greatly.

Working to *understand* risk attitudes is a worthwhile exercise on its own, but it is infinitely more valuable when combined with practical ways to *manage* those risk attitudes so that they support achievement of objectives. We know the insights contained within this book work in practice – we hope that readers will be motivated to prove that for themselves.

DAVID HILLSON
RUTH MURRAY-WEBSTER

Preface

Risk management is recognized as an essential contributor to business and project success, since it focuses on addressing uncertainties in a proactive manner in order to minimize threats, maximize opportunities and optimize achievement of objectives. There is wide convergence and international consensus on the necessary elements for a risk management process, and this is supported by a growing range of capable tools and techniques, an accepted body of knowledge, an academic and research base, and wide experience of practical implementation across many industries.

Despite this vision, in practice risk management often fails to meet expectations, as demonstrated by the continued history of business and project failures. Foreseeable threats materialize into problems and crises, and achievable opportunities are missed leading to lost benefits. Clearly the mere existence of accepted principles, well-defined processes and widespread practice is not sufficient to guarantee success. Some other essential ingredient is missing.

The most significant Critical Success Factor for effective risk management is the one most often lacking: an appropriate and mature risk culture. Research and experience both indicate that the attitude of individuals and organizations has a significant influence on whether risk management delivers what it promises. Risk management is undertaken by people acting individually and in various groups. The human element introduces an additional layer of complexity into the risk process, with a multitude of influences both explicit and covert. These lead to adoption of risk attitudes which affect every aspect of risk management. Risk attitudes exist at individual, group, corporate and national levels, and can be assessed and described with some degree of accuracy, allowing sources of bias to be diagnosed, exposing their influence on the risk process.

But diagnosis is different from cure. Where the risk attitude currently adopted by an individual or group is not conducive to effective risk management, action may be required to modify that attitude. Recent advances in the field of emotional intelligence and emotional literacy provide a means by which attitudinal change can be promoted and managed, for both individuals and organizations.

This book brings together leading-edge thinking on risk attitudes and emotional literacy to guide those wishing to move beyond mere implementation of a risk process and towards a people-centred approach for risk management. It offers a unique framework for understanding and managing those human elements which are essential for effective risk management. The combination generates powerful insights into how the application of emotional literacy to risk psychology can deliver significant benefits to every business seeking to manage uncertainty and its effects.

Following the thesis offered here requires no prior knowledge of emotional literacy, since this is a relatively new field, neither is understanding of risk attitudes or psychology assumed. However, the reader should be familiar with the purpose and basic processes of risk management – such knowledge is readily available and there are many books already published on this subject.

Instead, the main aim of this book is to provide a thought-provoking but usable reference for risk practitioners, enabling them to consider and manage the impacts of the human dimension on risk management. This will allow risk professionals to diagnose practically real situations and develop strategies for good practice, as well as minimising the impact of situations where current risk attitudes may be counter-productive.

Anyone involved with implementing risk management will benefit from this book, including risk practitioners, senior managers and directors responsible for corporate governance, project managers and their teams. It will also be of interest to human resource professionals and others interested in organizational or behavioural psychology, as well as students, researchers and practitioners in the field of emotional literacy, although the approach is pragmatic rather than theoretical or research-based. Indeed anyone whose interests include both the effective management of risk and the complexity of human behaviour will find much of value here, covering each of these two fascinating topics, but more particularly dealing with their interaction. If the goal is both to understand and to manage risk attitude, this book points the way.

DAVID HILLSON
RUTH MURRAY-WEBSTER

Acknowledgements

'Two are better than one because they have a good reward for their toil
... A threefold cord is not quickly broken': *King Solomon (970–928 BC)*.

When we set out to write the first edition of this book together it was based on mutual respect and appreciation, both professional and personal. When the task was completed we were pleased to acknowledge the privilege of working with each other (and we were still friends!). Each learned from the other's area of expertise, producing a natural synergy where the whole book was greater than the sum of our individual contributions. More interesting for the topic was our experience as two individuals of understanding our risk attitudes better and developing improved emotional literacy through the writing process. And as a minimal working group of two, we demonstrated that the principles outlined in this book work in practice.

Many people contributed to our thinking as reflected here – too many to name individually. We remain grateful to the many whose own experience added to our understanding of how to manage risk attitudes using the techniques of emotional literacy. Some have shown us how it should be done, and we have learned how not to do it from others. Where specific ideas have been derived from elsewhere we have attempted to give full acknowledgement, but we retain responsibility (and apologise) for any errors or oversights in our work.

Few situations contain more risk or demand more emotional literacy than the home, and our families have continued to teach us valuable lessons with broader application than the business environment. Our first edition would not have been written without their faithful support and encouragement.

Now we come to a second edition we have more reasons to be grateful. Firstly we thank the many people who read the first edition and provided valuable comment and feedback. Their input has shaped the changes in this edition, as well as challenging us to continue developing our ideas and writing. Secondly we are grateful to professional colleagues whose encouragement and support has provided the stimulus for us to keep going. We thank our publisher Jonathan Norman and his team at Gower for keeping faith with us and giving us opportunities to share our ideas more widely. And lastly, we acknowledge the strategic support of key people who have demonstrated their belief in our message by introducing us to unexpected avenues where we might make a difference. Baroness Julia Neuberger has been a particular encouragement in this respect.

We remain fascinated by the twin challenges of understanding uncertainty and understanding people, and we hope that the fruit of our labours continues to shed light on both.

DAVID HILLSON
RUTH MURRAY-WEBSTER
Petersfield & Meltham, UK
2007

PART 1

The Problem

CHAPTER 1

Risk Management Status Quo – Efficient but not Effective?

THE RISK ENVIRONMENT

The Danish Nobel Prize-winning physicist Niels Bohr (1885–1962) rightly said that 'Prediction is very difficult, especially about the future.' And yet people constantly seek to look ahead in an attempt to see what might be coming, to prepare themselves to respond appropriately and to be best positioned for all eventualities. This is true of individuals, families, communities, teams, organizations, businesses and nations. Each tries in different ways to predict the future for their own advantage. This may be a unique characteristic of humans as we attempt to make sense of our environment and our place within it, since forward planning seems to be both an innate skill and a psychological necessity that features in nearly all human activity.

The key factor underlying the difficulty in predicting the future is the existence of *uncertainty*. As Plato (427–347 BC) realized, 'The problem with the future is that more things might happen than will happen.' With an infinite number of possibilities ahead, it is hardly surprising that the task of selecting the one which will eventually materialize is problematic. And as the time horizon of prediction extends further into the future, the number of degrees of freedom increases exponentially, further complicating the ability to predict. In the desire to increase predictability, considerable attention has therefore been paid to defining, understanding and managing uncertainty. Many philosophers, theologians and scientists through the ages have addressed this issue, taking a range of different approaches to the problem, and arriving at significantly different proposed responses and solutions. At one extreme is the suggestion that the universe is inherently unknowable, ineffable and 'other', so the search for understanding, certainty or predictability is futile. The other extreme holds that advances in human science and technology constantly reduce the scope of uncertainty, improving the ability to understand and predict the behaviour of the observed universe, and that ongoing discoveries will continue this trend.

It is neither possible nor desirable to detail here the full scope of the debate on the nature of uncertainty. It is, however, useful to distinguish two key elements which contribute to uncertainty, since these are fundamentally different, and require managing in different ways. These two aspects of uncertainty are *variability* and *ambiguity*.

- *Variability* refers to the situation when a measurable factor can take one of a range of possible values. The classic example is dice. Each die has six faces marked 1–6, and a throw always results in one side facing upwards. There is no doubt that the result will be one of the numbers 1–6, and the chance of any particular number resulting from a throw is one in six, but the precise value of the result for a given throw is not predictable in advance (assuming the die is fair and unbiased). This type of uncertainty is known as *aleatoric*, from the Latin *alea* (a game of chance using dice). The event is defined but its outcome is uncertain because it is variable.

- *Ambiguity* is defined on the other hand as uncertainty of meaning. It can be used about whether or not a particular event will happen at all, or whether something else unforeseen might occur. Here the issue is not the probability of an event producing a particular value from within a known range; instead there is uncertainty about the event itself, with lack of clarity over some aspect of its existence, content or meaning. This type of uncertainty is described as *epistemic* (from the Greek *episteme*, meaning knowledge), since there is incomplete knowledge about the situation under consideration.

Both variability and ambiguity must be recognized and actively managed if the task of predicting the future is to be attempted. These two types of uncertainty exist in all areas of life, and humans react to them in a variety of ways. Human behaviour in the presence of uncertainty is not always rational, but efforts can and should be made to understand the possible range of such behaviours so that they can be managed appropriately. This book aims to make a significant and positive contribution to creating such understanding by addressing the specific question of *risk attitudes*.

This introduces two more terms which deserve careful definition, namely *risk* and *attitude*. These are addressed in the next two sections.

WHAT IS RISK?

Risk is not the same as uncertainty, so how are the two related? The word 'risk' is a common and widely used part of today's vocabulary, relating to personal circumstances (health, pensions, insurance, investments and so on), society (terrorism, economic performance, food safety and so on), and business (corporate governance, strategy, business continuity and so on). Yet, somewhat surprisingly, there is still no broad consensus on the meaning of this term. Various national and international standards and guidelines exist which mention risk, but there are many different definitions and underlying concepts in these documents. Even among risk practitioners in the various professional bodies there is an ongoing debate about the subject matter at the heart of their discipline. And of course there is huge variation in the general literature, reflecting the lack of official agreement on the basic definition of risk.

Despite differences of detail, all definitions agree that risk has two characteristics: it is related to *uncertainty*, and it has *consequences*. Risk, however, is not the same as uncertainty, whether aleatoric variability or epistemic ambiguity. The key distinction between uncertainty and risk arises from consideration of the consequences. Perhaps the simplest definition of risk is 'uncertainty that matters', since uncertainty without consequence poses no risk. In this sense, risk cannot be defined unless it is related to objectives of some kind.

A more complete definition of risk would therefore be 'an uncertainty that could affect one or more objectives'. This recognizes the fact that there are some uncertainties that do not matter in the relevant context. For example a particular child may be taking an examination tomorrow with an uncertain (variable) outcome (that is pass or fail), but this has little or no impact on anyone outside the child, the family and the school. To most people the exam result is an uncertainty that does not matter, and so it is not a risk. Uncertainty (ambiguity) about whether or not it will rain heavily in Kazakhstan tomorrow is irrelevant to the majority of businesses or individuals, so this too does not pose a risk. If, however, the child is a Kazakh and his father has promised a fishing trip as a reward for passing the exam, both uncertainties become relevant in the context, and represent risks to the desired objective of going fishing tomorrow after a successful exam result.

Linking risk with objectives makes it clear that every facet of life is risky. All types of human endeavour are undertaken in order to achieve objectives of some sort, including personal and informal objectives (for example to be happy and healthy), project objectives (including delivering on time and within budget) and corporate business objectives (such as to increase profit and market share). Since the environment within which these human endeavours are undertaken is inherently uncertain, it follows that wherever objectives are defined, there will be risks to their successful achievement.

Defining this link between risk and objectives is essential to the process of risk management, since it is a prerequisite for identifying risks, assessing their significance and determining appropriate responses. It is also, however, a crucial factor in understanding risk attitudes, since these are driven by the objectives of the individual, group or organization concerned, and the extent to which the risk 'matters'.

Another interesting trend emerges from the definition debate when the various official published risk management standards are examined. This also arises from the concept of risk as 'uncertainty that matters', since it relates to the nature of the consequence.

- Before 1997, all official published risk management standards used an exclusively negative definition of risk, with the term being synonymous with danger, hazard, loss and so on. In these definitions, risk was seen as 'an uncertainty that could have a negative/harmful/adverse/unwelcome/bad effect on one or more objectives', that is, risk equals threat.

- From 1997 onwards, standards publications started to appear which presented either a neutral risk definition of 'an uncertainty that could affect one or more objectives' (where the type of impact is undefined), or a broad definition including both downside and upside impact: 'an uncertainty that could have a positive or negative effect on one or more objectives'. These give a definition of risk including both negative threats as well as positive opportunities.

- Since 2000 the clear majority of newly published or updated official standards relating to risk management have explicitly treated risk as including both threats and opportunities.

Although the definition debate is continuing and not all risk practitioners agree, adoption of a widened concept of risk seems to be growing. There is increasing awareness that risk management can and should be used to minimize the negative effect of downside threat-risks, while also attempting to maximize the positive effect of upside opportunity-risks, in order to optimize achievement of objectives.

For the purposes of this book, the broader definition of risk is used. This is not simply to reflect the current trend in the definition debate. It is also relevant to the subject of risk attitudes, since the *perception of risk* is a key driver of attitude to risk. Clearly people who see risk as wholly negative will have a different approach to it from those who are also aware of potential upside. The recognition of opportunities which can be proactively managed is a significant influence on risk attitude, and it can also provide a powerful motivation for attitudinal management and modification.

WHAT IS ATTITUDE?

Attitude is another word used commonly but loosely, and in a book dealing with risk attitudes it is essential that this too is clearly defined. Dictionaries offer two differing definitions. The first relates to the inner working of the human mind, where 'attitude' is 'state of mind, mental view or disposition with regard to a fact or state'. A second equally valid definition describes the positioning of an object in space, such as an aircraft, spaceship, or missile, where 'attitude' is said to mean 'orientation of axes in relation to some reference plane, usually the horizontal'.

It is interesting to note that both definitions insist that attitude can only exist in relation to a datum point – either a fact towards which one holds a mental disposition, or a reference plane such as the horizon against which orientation is measured. In this respect 'attitude' is similar to 'risk', which is defined in terms of objectives.

Although at first sight mental views and aircraft positioning do not seem to have much in common, in fact the two definitions of attitude are not incompatible or unrelated. The second meaning gives the sense of attitude as describing 'direction of lean'. This can be seen as a metaphor for the internal approach adopted by an individual or group towards a given situation, and a number of useful insights arise as corollaries of this view, with each individual or group being the pilot of their own attitudinal aircraft.

- Just as the pilot makes a decision on what attitude to adopt for the aircraft in three-dimensional space in order to position it to execute the desired manoeuvre, so an individual or group can make an attitudinal choice to lean towards a particular desired response, behaviour or outcome.

- The attitude of an aircraft does not in itself result in motion, although it is a direct influence on the direction taken. In addition to attitude some force must act on the aircraft to generate motion – analogous to motivation.

- Aircraft attitude needs to be followed by movement if it is to result in execution of a manoeuvre, and similarly individual or group attitudes must be translated into action if the desired outcome is to be achieved.

- Attitude in space can be described using a number of elements, usually termed 'pitch' (rotation about the axis from wing tip to wing tip), 'roll' (rotation about the axis from nose to tail) and 'yaw' (rotation about the axis from ceiling to floor). It is also possible to subdivide human attitudes into their component dimensions to enable them to be better understood and managed.

- As the number of degrees of freedom for aircraft movement is almost unlimited within the three dimensions of space, so there is a bewildering array of potential attitudes that can be chosen in any given situation.

- It is possible for extremes of attitude to make an aircraft unstable (for example stall or spin), resulting in loss of control and potentially catastrophic consequences. Similarly a sense of balance is required for individuals and groups if their attitudes are not to lead to undesired outcomes.

- Different extremes of attitude require different types of response. For example if an aircraft finds itself in a stall (resulting from a lack of laminar flow over the aircraft's wings when the angle between the aircraft's direction of motion and the direction of air flow is too high), the correct response is to do nothing, allowing the aircraft to self-correct. In the case of spin, however, (where there is a lack of laminar flow over the aircraft's wings and the aircraft is rotating about its yaw axis) emergency action is required to bring the aircraft under control. In the same way some extremes of human attitude are self-correcting where others require aggressive intervention.

- While there may be a preferred response (initial default positioning), the final outcome remains a matter of choice.

As a result of this comparison, the term 'attitude' as applied to internal human mental processes and positioning is used here to refer to *chosen responses* to situations. Some attitudes may be deeply rooted, representing core values for the individual or group, but they nevertheless represent a choice. Other attitudes may be more malleable. Attitudes differ from personal characteristics in that they are situational responses rather than natural preferences or traits, and chosen attitudes may therefore differ depending on a range of different influences. *Perception* is also a key driver of attitude, since this determines how a particular situation is seen, and hence the chosen response which is considered to be appropriate. Clearly if these influences can be identified and understood, the possibility of changing them is introduced, allowing individuals and groups to manage their attitudes proactively – which is the basis of emotional literacy.

The fact that attitudes can be modified is essential to the case for *understanding and managing risk attitudes*. If attitudes were fixed inherent attributes of individuals, inborn and unchangeable, then while it might be possible to *understand* them it would never be possible to *manage* them. The attitudes of individuals or groups would then not be comparable to an aircraft flying freely through the air, but would instead be like a cruise missile pre-programmed to strike a fixed target.

The best that could be achieved with fixed attitudes would be to react or respond to their presence. The fact that some people act as if their attitudes were indeed fixed ('It's just the way I am and I can't help it') does not change the reality that attitudes are chosen, even if the choice is made at a deep level of consciousness not evident to the individual. The first objective of *understanding* attitudes in general, and risk attitudes in particular, is necessary in order to achieve the second objective of being able to *manage* them proactively and intelligently.

The way in which individuals and groups choose or adopt attitudes in situations of uncertainty is addressed in more detail in Part 2, and options for modifying these choices using emotional literacy approaches are presented in Part 4.

RISK MANAGEMENT IN TODAY'S BUSINESS

Given its significance in facilitating achievement of objectives, the structured application of risk management in the world of business has become increasingly widespread. Risk management has become recognized as a management discipline in its own right, with a broad supporting infrastructure. Elements of this support include:

- *Academic base.* Many universities and educational establishments offer basic and advanced teaching in risk management, at degree, masters and doctoral levels, and both theoretical and applied research programmes are also available.

- *Literature.* In addition to the wide range of national and international risk management standards and guidelines, there is a number of refereed journals covering the topic, as well as a huge variety of books on various aspects of risk.

- *Process.* Over time a broad consensus has developed on the elements required for an effective risk process, including an initial planning phase to define the context, followed by risk identification, assessment and prioritization using qualitative and quantitative methods, development of appropriate responses, implementation of agreed actions, risk communication and review.

- *Professional bodies.* Many professional societies exist specifically to promote and support the discipline of risk management. Among the most prominent are the Institute of Risk Management (IRM) and the Association of Insurance and Risk Managers (AIRMIC) in the UK, the Global Association of Risk Professionals (GARP), the Public Risk Management Association (PRIMA), the Risk Management Association (RMA), the Federation of European Risk Management Associations (FERMA), the European Institute of Risk Management (EIRM) and the Society for Risk Analysis (SRA). Other professional bodies in different sectors also have specific interest groups (SIGs) covering risk management, for example the Project Management Institute (PMI), the UK Association for Project Management (APM), the International Association of Contract and Commercial Managers (IACCM), the International Council on Systems Engineering (INCOSE), the Insurance Information Institute (III), the Insurance Institute of America (IIA), the Risk Management Institution of Australasia (RMIA) and the Professional Risk Managers' International Association (PRMIA). [Website addresses for these organizations are given at the end of this chapter.]

- *Qualifications.* A range of examinations and qualifications are available for the risk professional, though there is no clear consensus on a single certification which is recognized across all industries or countries. In addition to academic qualifications available through universities, it is now possible to become a Certified Risk Professional (see www.bai.org/CRP), a Certified Practicing Risk Manager or a Professional Risk Manager (see prmia.org/certification/cert.php), a Finance Risk Manager (see www.GARP.com/FRMexam), or an Associate in Risk Management (see www.aicpcu.org/flyers/ARM.htm), or to take examinations leading to the IRM Diploma in Risk Management or the APM Project Risk Management Certificate (also available through IRM).

- *Tools.* Software vendors offer a wide variety of tools to support all aspects of the risk process, as well as specialized tools for particular applications. There is also a growing market in enterprise risk management solutions, providing an integrated approach to managing risk across the organization. The current generation of risk tools have powerful functionality, good user interfaces and increasing integration capability.

- *Consultancies.* Solution providers also offer risk management support, allowing clients to benefit from their expertise and experience, and sharing best practice thinking and practical implementation. The growth in popularity of risk management has increased the number of consultancies offering support in this area, though purchasers of risk support services need to exercise discretion in selecting suppliers with genuine ability rather than marketing hype.

In parallel to development of a substantial infrastructure to support implementation of risk management, application of risk processes has reached ever further across the boundaries of business. Risk management is not only practised formally in most industries, in many countries, and in both government and the private sector, but it also plays an important role at all levels in organizations. The types of risk addressed in businesses include the following:

- corporate governance

- business risk

- reputation risk

- business continuity

- disaster recovery

- strategic risk

- financial/credit/treasury risk

- country risk

- political risk

- information security

- fraud risk

- market risk

- project risk

- operational risk

- technical risk

- health and safety

- environmental risk.

This breadth of application emphasizes the need for a joined-up approach to risk management which is holistic and integrated across all levels of the organization, including implementation of the risk process and its supporting infrastructure. As a result of this wide-ranging scope of risk affecting the entire business, risk management needs to be fully effective in order to meet the challenge.

IS RISK MANAGEMENT EFFECTIVE?

Efficiency describes the application of resources to inputs in order to generate outputs with minimal waste. *Effectiveness* on the other hand is not just about the ratio of input to output, but instead relates to the extent to which a measurable result is obtained. It is clear that risk management success should be determined in terms of effectiveness rather than mere efficiency, since the very purpose of risk management is to maximize achievement of objectives.

The preceding section in this chapter has shown that awareness and application of risk management has penetrated widely into the world of business, and it is now seen as a key contributor to business and project success. Risk management tools, techniques and processes are being implemented with increasing efficiency as organizations seek to reap the promised rewards of proactively addressing the effects of uncertainty on achievement of objectives.

However, despite this recognition of the role of risk management, businesses still struggle, surprises still occur, projects still fail and the future remains unpredictable. In other words, risk management as commonly implemented may be *efficient*, using the processes, tools and techniques with little wasted effort, but it is often not *effective*, not achieving the set objectives or delivering the promised benefits. This is not to say that risk management can change the inherently uncertain nature of the future; rather that it should improve the ability of individuals and organizations to predict and manage future uncertainty. And yet experience continues to demonstrate otherwise.

Why should this be? Is it the result of some failure of risk management in principle, with a flawed concept or theory? Or perhaps the process is faulty, and is not adequate to the challenge of exposing and addressing uncertainty? Maybe staff are not being properly trained in how to apply risk management, or the tools are not up to the job?

The risk literature discusses a number of Critical Success Factors (CSFs) which have the potential to influence risk management effectiveness. The broad conclusion is that nothing is wrong with the concepts or theory, and that inadequate tools, techniques or training cannot bear the whole blame for lack of risk management effectiveness. Instead the problem lies in how risk management is actually implemented.

Most commentators agree that the most significant CSF influencing effective risk management implementation is the one most often lacking: an appropriate and mature risk culture. Research and experience both indicate that the attitude of individuals and organizations towards risk has a significant influence on whether risk management delivers what it promises. Risk management is undertaken by people, acting individually and in various groups. Each group exercises a greater or lesser degree of influence over others, with varying levels of overlap, creating complex hierarchical sets of membership and influence, as summarized in Figure 1.1.

Figure 1.1   Hierarchies of membership and influence (not to scale)

The human element introduces an additional layer of complexity into the risk process, with a multitude of influences both explicit and covert. These act as sources of bias, creating preferred risk attitudes which affect every aspect of risk management. This issue is explored further in Chapter 2, where the importance of human factors in the risk process is examined in detail.

Risk attitudes exist at individual, group, corporate and national levels, and attempts can be made to assess and describe them. This allows sources of bias to be diagnosed, exposing their influence on the risk process. Diagnosis should then lead on to treatment, taking action to modify risk attitudes where the existing situation is not conducive to effective risk management.

PURPOSE AND STRUCTURE OF THIS BOOK

The human aspects of risk management are acknowledged as being critical to success, but very little has been written about what this really means in practice, or about how to manage proactively the influence of human behaviour on the risk process. A people-centred approach for risk management would address this issue and allow risk attitudes to be both understood and managed. This would provide practical guidelines allowing individuals, senior managers and risk professionals to diagnose real situations and develop strategies for good practice, as well as minimizing the impact of situations where risk attitudes may be counter-productive.

This book is designed to define and bridge this gap. Having introduced in Part 1 the current status of risk management and outlined why human factors matter, Part 2 that follows defines and details the range of possible risk attitudes, looking both at individuals and groups. This is followed in Part 3 by a review of recent advances in the field of emotional intelligence and emotional literacy, which provide a means by which attitudinal change can be promoted and managed, for both individuals and organizations.

Finally the two areas are brought together in Part 4, applying the insights of emotional literacy to the field of risk attitudes. This is presented in a practical and applied framework rather than as a theoretical or academic treatise, based on the authors' shared experiences and expertise rather than on empirical research. This combination of two leading-edge areas creates a uniquely powerful approach allowing risk attitudes to be understood and managed, and so addresses the most common shortfall in risk management implementation: failure to manage the human aspects of the risk process. The reasons why these aspects are important to risk management effectiveness are addressed in the next chapter.

Web addresses for professional bodies related to risk management:

- UK Institute of Risk Management (IRM) www.theIRM.org

- UK Association of Insurance and Risk Managers (AIRMIC) www.AIRMIC.com

- Global Association of Risk Professionals (GARP) www.GARP.com

- Public Risk Management Association (PRIMA) www.PRIMAcentral.org

- Risk Management Association (RMA) www.RMAhq.org

- Federation of European Risk Management Associations (FERMA) www.ferma-asso.org

- European Institute of Risk Management (EIRM) www.EIRM.com

- Society for Risk Analysis (SRA) www.sra.org

- Project Management Institute Risk Management Specific Interest Group (PMI Risk SIG) www.RiskSIG.com

- UK APM Risk SIG www.apm.org.uk/riskmanagement.asp

- International Association of Contract and Commercial Managers (IACCM) Risk Working Group www.IACCM.com

- International Council on Systems Engineering (INCOSE) Risk Management Working Party www.INCOSE.org/practice/techactivities/wg.risk

- Insurance Information Institute (III) www.iii.org

- Insurance Institute of America (ITA) www.aicpcu.org

- Risk Management Institution of Australasia (RMIA) www.rmia.org.au

- Professional Risk Managers' International Association (PRMIA) http://prmia.org

CHAPTER 2

The Importance of Human Factors in Risk Management

Every area of endeavour has a number of elements which must be present for it to be undertaken. But many of these are 'necessary but not sufficient', in other words they are factors which are essential but which are not the main key contributors to success. An influence which directly determines whether or not the endeavour succeeds is called a Critical Success Factor. A CSF is something which really matters. If it is present the endeavour is more likely to succeed, but if it is absent the chances of failure are significantly increased.

A number of CSFs have been identified for risk management. These are listed in Table 2.1 (not in order of importance or priority). From these, there is general agreement among risk practitioners and users of risk management services about the most significant CSF. This is usually called 'human factors', though the phrase needs careful definition. It originated in scientific studies of the human-machine interface, particularly in the field of ergonomics though more recently encompassing psychological aspects; and the concept was then expanded to refer to individual, group and organizational factors which can affect safety at work. Most recently human

Table 2.1 Critical Success Factors for effective risk management

Shared understanding of key concepts and principles of risk management
Agreed definitions of key risk management terms, common language
Simple and scaleable process for risk management
Efficient procedural framework to support the risk process
Proven methods and techniques to implement all elements of the risk process
Capable tools to support risk techniques
Skilled and experienced staff to contribute to the risk process
Clear objectives for risk management, at business, strategic and project levels
Availability of adequate resources for implementation of the risk process (human, financial, technical, organizational and so on)
Availability of adequate resources for implementation of agreed risk responses
Buy-in from all stakeholders in the risk process, including agreement to contribute inputs where required, and commitment to use outputs
Risk-aware organizational culture, which recognizes the existence of uncertainty in business and projects and determines to address it proactively
Acceptance of the need to change in response to risk, at both strategic and tactical levels
Suitable contractual framework to facilitate the risk process

factors have been defined as 'individual, group and organizational factors which influence the behaviour of people and the work environment in a way which can affect achievement of objectives', and this broader approach is the one followed here. It is interesting to note that, like definitions of 'risk' and 'attitude' discussed in Chapter 1, 'human factors' can only be defined in relation to objectives. This begins to make clear the link between human factors, risk and attitude, since all three relate to achievement of defined objectives.

The 'factors' encompassed by the above definition can be described at three levels:

- *Individual factors*, such as competence, capability, skills, knowledge, stress levels, motivation, emotional health, cultural background and so on.

- *Group factors*, including interpersonal issues, leadership style, hierarchical power, communication approach, coordination, supervision, empowerment, task focus and so on.

- *Organizational factors*, like corporate ethos, policies, standards, previous experience, market positioning, senior management style, systems and procedures, and so on.

Given the range of possible interpretations for the term 'human factors', other names have become common, such as people aspects, soft elements, the cultural dimension and so on. Whatever name is used, the point remains that people are the most important contributor to risk management effectiveness, for both good and ill. There is a number of reasons for this, at both personal and corporate levels, explored further below.

But whether human factors are considered for individuals or groups, the main reason that this affects the risk management process is the influence of risk attitudes. It is important to recognize that risk attitudes do not only exist in the heads and hearts of individuals. Groups of people also hold identifiable attitudes towards risk, which are not necessarily the sum or average of the risk attitudes of the constituent individuals. And corporate risk attitude drives action at the group level, especially decision-making, as surely as individual actions are influenced by personal risk attitude.

Both personal and corporate risk attitudes are considered in more detail in Part 2 of this book. But before undertaking a detailed examination of risk attitudes, it is important to understand why they are important in the context of the risk management process. Surely if risk management is well understood, with clear principles, defined processes, user-friendly tools, efficient techniques, trained and skilled people, and so on, then its implementation should not be variable. Applying the standard approach to managing risk should deliver results every time.

Experience tells a different story: despite the presence of all the 'necessary but not sufficient' elements such as processes, tools, techniques and training, lack of understanding and management of the soft side of risk management can sabotage the process and lead to ineffectiveness. Why is this the case?

WHY HUMAN FACTORS MATTER TO RISK MANAGEMENT

Risk management is not done by machines or robots. The reason is simple – it requires human judgement. It is not a question of mathematical calculation or measurement, neither is it a case of straightforward extrapolation from input data using well-defined rules to generate unambiguous outputs. Consequently risk management cannot be undertaken mechanistically, although automated tools are very useful in handling large amounts of data, and in performing complex calculations rapidly and reliably.

In fact one of the main benefits of a structured approach to risk management is that it provides a framework for application of human factors to the process of managing businesses and projects. This includes judgement, insights, intuition, previous experiences and so on, all of which provide a rich source of additional information about the risks faced by the project or business. To ignore these inputs would impoverish risk management and limit it to dry considerations of measurable facts. Human factors represent an important aspect of the risk process, particularly in risk identification, risk assessment and risk response development.

It is vital to recognize that all contributions made by human factors to the risk management process are affected by those characteristics which distinguish human beings from machines (and indeed from animals). While this is an enormous topic spanning psychology, physiology, sociology, anthropology, philosophy and so on, the discussion in this book is limited to the specific area of attitudes, and most particularly attitudes towards risk. But before going on to consider these in detail in Part 2, it is important to reflect on how human factors can affect the risk management process. It is useful to separate this into two elements: the influence of individuals on risk management, and the behaviour of groups.

RISK MANAGEMENT AND THE INDIVIDUAL

The entire risk management process is undertaken by people, acting either individually or in groups. The key influencing factor, however, is the individual, since groups are made up of individuals making their own contributions in the form of data, information, choices, decisions, opinions and actions. As a result it is essential to

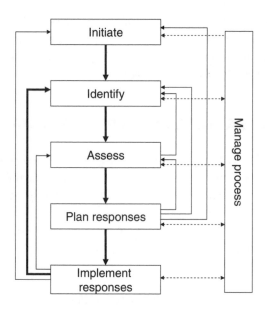

Figure 2.1   Typical risk management process (based on APM, 2004)

understand the effects which the attitudes of individuals can have on the risk process, in order to be able to move on to manage these effects appropriately.

Individuals contribute to the risk management process in many ways, each of which is affected by their risk attitude. A typical risk process is described in Figure 2.1, with the following stages:

- First is an **initiation** phase, ensuring that objectives are agreed and understood by all stakeholders, and determining the level of detail required for the risk process, driven by the perceived riskiness and strategic importance of the project or business area under consideration.

- After definition is risk **identification**, using techniques such as brainstorms, workshops, checklists, prompt lists, interviews, questionnaires and so on. Here, care is needed to distinguish between risks and related non-risks (for example problems, issues, causes and effects).

- The significance of identified risks needs to be **assessed**, prioritizing key risks for further attention and action. Assessment can be *qualitative* (describing characteristics of each risk in sufficient detail to allow them to be understood), or *quantitative* (using mathematical models to simulate the effect of risks on project outcomes).

- Next comes **response planning**, when strategies and actions are determined to deal with risks in a way that is *appropriate, achievable* and *affordable*. Each action should be *agreed* with stakeholders and *allocated* to an owner, then its effectiveness should be *assessed*.

- Planning must lead to action, so it is important to implement planned actions, monitor effectiveness and report results to stakeholders. During this **implementation** phase, risk exposure is actually modified as a result of taking suitable action.

- Lastly, there must be a **process management** step, including reviews and updates. Risk is always changing so the process must be cyclic, regularly reviewing risk exposure, identifying and assessing new risks, and ensuring appropriate responses.

Figure 2.1 shows that the risk management process is highly iterative, with each stage potentially leading back to previous stages. The main update cycle is shown with thicker arrows in the figure, with internal process cycles shown lighter.

Before considering the contributions of individuals to each of these stages, a preliminary outline of risk attitudes is necessary at this point. This subject is discussed in detail in Part 2, but here it is sufficient simply to state that individual risk attitudes exist on a spectrum, ranging from people who are very uncomfortable in the presence of uncertainty ('risk-averse') through to those who view uncertainty as a welcome challenge ('risk-seeking'). This spectrum is a continuum, and although it is convenient for diagnostic and didactic purposes to identify and label a small number of representative states along the spectrum, it must be recognized that each person is a complex individual whose attitudes may defy simple categorization. Nevertheless when outlining the influence of individuals on the risk management process, such labels offer a useful shorthand.

It is also important to realize that a person's risk attitude is not fixed. There are many factors which influence the risk attitude of individuals, and these are discussed in Chapters 3 and 4. This section considers the ways in which individual risk attitudes exert an influence on the risk process itself (group influences are discussed later in this chapter).

So how do the 'soft factors' of individuals affect the risk process? What difference does one particular person's input make to risk management as opposed to the contribution of another? At each stage in the risk process, different individual risk attitudes can lead to very different outcomes. This is discussed in the following paragraphs and summarized in Table 2.2, using the shorthand labels 'risk-averse' and 'risk-seeking' to represent two points at either end of the risk attitude spectrum.

Table 2.2 Influence of individual risk attitudes on risk management process

Process stage (main aim)	Influence of risk-aversion	Influence of risk-seeking
INITIATION OF RISK PROCESS Set appropriate level of detail for risk process based on perceived riskiness and strategic importance	Oversensitive to negative risks (threats), but not prepared to pursue positive risks (opportunities). Prefer detailed or intensive risk process to respond to perception of higher risk. Not confident in ability of normal processes to deal with level of risk faced.	Tendency to downplay negative risks (threats) and be optimistic about positive risks (opportunities). Prefer informal risk process since risk exposure perceived as low. Confident that normal processes can cope with any risks that may arise.
RISK IDENTIFICATION Identify all foreseeable uncertainties with the potential to affect objectives	Pessimism. Identification of many threats, including insignificant ones that may not deserve attention, or obscure ones that are unlikely to occur. Overlook opportunities.	Optimism. Unaware or unconcerned about threats, treating them as 'business as usual' rather than specific items to be addressed by risk process. Tendency to overplay opportunities.
QUALITATIVE RISK ASSESSMENT Prioritize identified risks for further attention and action	Focus on impact rather than probability. Threats are seen as potentially severe, but any opportunities will only be small. Overall assessment leads to many major threats and a few small opportunities.	Focus on probability rather than impact. Threats are unlikely whereas opportunities are probable. Overall assessment leads to few minor threats and significant opportunities.
QUANTITATIVE RISK ANALYSIS Develop models to analyze effect of risks on overall outcome	Input data has wide ranges, especially on down-side, reflecting significant uncertainty. High worst-case estimates for threats, with high max figures in 3-point estimates. Best-case close to most-likely for opportunities, reflecting lack of confidence in ability to create additional benefits. Cautious or pessimistic interpretation of analytical outputs.	Input data has narrow ranges reflecting confidence in plan and ability to manage. Reduced worst-case estimates for threats, with low max figures in 3-point estimates. Best-case significantly lower than most-likely for opportunities, reflecting confidence in ability to exploit them. Optimistic interpretation of analytical outputs.

Continued

Table 2.2 *Concluded*

Process stage (main aim)	Influence of risk-aversion	Influence of risk-seeking
RISK RESPONSE PLANNING Select appropriate risk responses strategies and agree actions	Prefer aggressive responses for threats (avoidance, minimization, transfer). Welcome risk transfer options for threats, and tend to abdicate responsibility once transfer is agreed. Under-reaction to opportunities or ignore them.	Accept threats passively, or ignore them, relying on contingency plans or reactive actions if threats materialize. Regard risk transfer of threats as a sign of weakness or inadequancy. Select aggressive responses for opportunities (exploit, capture, maximize).
IMPLEMENTATION Take actions as planned and monitor effectiveness	Seek immediate implementation of agreed responses. Conscientious about completing actions. Tendency to gold-plate responses 'just in case'. Report high levels of threats, downplay opportunities and recommend proaction action.	Relaxed attitude to implementing responses. Lack of commitment to perform proactive actions. Tendency to take short-cuts. Report good chance of success, with low threat levels and significant opportunities for improvement.
PROCESS MANAGEMENT Review and update risk information	High level of commitment to risk process. Regular provision of updated risk information, identifying new risks, participating in risk reviews and so on.	Low level of commitment to risk process. Failure to update risk information, identify new risks, or participate in risk reviews and so on.

INITIATION

Risk management is not a 'one-size-fits-all' process, and different depths of implementation are possible, depending on the particular requirements of the situation. In some circumstances it is enough to adopt an informal approach, passing rapidly through the various steps in the risk process, quickly identifying key risks and determining appropriate responses. This limited process might be suitable for a simple project or a situation which is similar to one encountered previously. Alternatively the organization may decide to implement a more detailed approach to risk management, spending significant time and effort to involve stakeholders in the process, using a variety of techniques to identify and analyze risks, with teams of specialists working to address the risks in detail. Such an in-depth approach could be appropriate for a highly innovative or complex project, or to deal with a business situation where the stakes are particularly high.

One of the main aims of the Initiation phase is to set an appropriate level of detail for the risk process, driven by perceived riskiness and strategic importance of the project or situation under consideration. The key word here is 'perceived', since perception can vary significantly between individuals. One may see a particular project or business decision as entirely straightforward and routine, not deserving any special attention. Another person may consider the same situation to be extremely risky and requiring a high degree of focused risk management.

Without understanding that these perspectives are driven by risk attitudes, the different viewpoints can be attributed to other factors such as seniority, experience or personality. This can lead to a decision on the amount of effort to be expended on the risk management process which is driven by unconscious attitudinal factors rather than by the reality of the situation. And an inappropriate risk process is likely to be inefficient or ineffective, either failing to meet the risk challenge if too little attention is given to risk management, or imposing unnecessary constraints and process bureaucracy if too high a process level is chosen.

RISK IDENTIFICATION

This stage seeks to identify all foreseeable uncertainties with the potential to affect objectives for better or worse. It is clear that an individual's attitude to uncertainty will have a significant influence over what is perceived to be a risk. Faced with the same situation, individuals with different risk attitudes will not identify the same set of risks. The extent to which a risk is 'foreseeable' depends on the filters that influence each individual's perception: some see through attitudinal 'magnifying glasses' that make risks appear to be larger or nearer, while others wear conceptual 'blinkers' that obscure visibility of risks and create blind-spots.

The risk-averse person who is uncomfortable in the presence of uncertainty is likely to be over-sensitized to negative risks (threats), and will tend to see them everywhere. They might also be expected to overlook potential opportunities, or see them as 'too risky'. This will result in identification of many threat-risks including insignificant ones that might perhaps not deserve attention, and missing opportunity-risks including those that could deliver significant additional benefits. Identifying a large number of risks can create 'noise' in the risk process, obscuring the major uncertainties that could affect achievement of objectives. It also leads to a high process overhead, since the significance of each identified risk must be assessed and appropriate responses must be determined. There may also be an impact on team morale if many of the risks passing through the process are seen to be 'too small to bother about'.

By contrast, risk-seeking individuals may fail to identify some real threats since they are not worried by uncertainty. They might also be tempted to over-play the importance of opportunities as these are seen as a challenge. There is a tendency to regard threat-risk as part of 'business as usual', and not deserving of special attention. Consequently a risk-seeking person may discount a number of threats which should receive proactive attention, viewing them as 'normal', and instead concentrate disproportionately on opportunities. The smaller number of identified negative risks and more positive ones may give the impression that the risk exposure of the project or business decision is lower than it really is, and lead to complacency or selection of an inappropriate strategy. It is also likely to reduce the effort applied to risk management, since the level of risk appears to be low. And of course if threats actually occur that were not identified, or expected opportunities fail to materialize, the validity and credibility of the risk process can be undermined.

RISK ASSESSMENT

Given a list of identified risks, the next step is to prioritize them for further attention and action. Assessment can be *qualitative* (describing characteristics of each risk in sufficient detail to allow them to be understood), or *quantitative* (using mathematical models to simulate the effect of risks on project outcomes). Assessment of both qualitative and quantitative prioritization criteria is driven by risk attitude, as outlined below:

- *Qualitative risk assessment* typically considers two dimensions for each risk: the probability that the risk might occur, and its potential impact on achievement of objectives if it did occur (recognizing that a risk can be either a threat with an adverse impact, or an opportunity with a beneficial impact). Risks are prioritized taking account of both dimensions, with high-probability/high-impact risks treated as top priority. Probability and impacts can be described using labels (high, medium, low and so on) or using numerical ranges such as 10–30 per cent for probability or 3–4 weeks for time impact (delay or saving). Even if the problems of defining terms are set aside, assessments of probability and impact for a given risk are inevitably subjective (unless there is relevant previous data or experience). Consequently, different risk attitudes will result in different assessments of the same risk. In the extreme, a risk-averse person would tend to overestimate both probability and impact of a given threat ('It's almost sure to happen and if it does it will be very bad'), and seek to downplay opportunities ('Better not take chances'). Risk-aversion also tends to lead to a preoccupation with impact rather than probability, since the individual is more concerned about what might happen that with how likely it is to occur. Risk-averse assessment results in many apparently major threats and a few small opportunities. On the other hand, a risk-seeking person is likely to underestimate threats ('Nothing to worry about'), and be optimistic about opportunities ('Too good to miss'). The focus is on probability (threats are unlikely, opportunities are highly probable), rather than impact. The resulting risk-seeking assessment in this case suggests few minor threats but significant opportunities – the precise converse of the assessment by a risk-averse person.

- *Quantitative risk analysis* involves developing models of the project or business situation into which the effects of risk are added. Computer-based simulations then indicate the range of possible outcomes, given the input data. Several quantitative techniques are commonly used, including decision trees, influence diagrams, Monte Carlo analysis, sensitivity analysis and so on. The operation of the various simulations is of course not influenced by the attitudes of individuals, since computerized tools merely perform defined transformations on input data to generate analytical outputs. There are, however, two distinct elements of quantitative analysis which are subject to the effects of risk attitudes – generation of input data and interpretation of outputs:

  - *Input.* As for qualitative assessments of probability and impact, data intended for input to quantitative risk models can be influenced by the risk attitude of the person preparing it. Risk-averse people produce wider ranges (reflecting more perceived uncertainty) and higher maximum figures (worst case) for threats, whereas risk-seekers have lower ranges and maxima. For opportunities the converse is true, with data from the risk-averse person indicating smaller potential benefits though still with a wide range of uncertainty, compared with the risk-seeking person whose view of opportunity leads to an enhanced best-case minimum and a reduced spread of uncertainty.

  - *Output.* Results from quantitative risk analyses require careful interpretation if they are to be used properly to support strategic or tactical decision-making. But interpretation is subject to the attitudes of the decision-maker, with a risk-averse person tending to be more cautious than the risk-seeking colleague.

RESPONSE PLANNING

The aim here is to select appropriate risk response strategies in order to minimize and avoid threats and to maximize and exploit opportunities. The influence of risk attitudes is evident in differing views of what is 'appropriate'.

Thus the risk-averse person will probably over-react and prefer aggressive responses to threat-risks, since they are particularly sensitive to these types of uncertainty and will seek to minimize or avoid them wherever possible. Risk transfer is seen as a good option for threats, since liability and ownership pass to a third party, but there is also a tendency to abdicate responsibility rather than retain it. Conversely the risk-averse response to opportunity-risks is usually to under-react, or even to ignore them, since the individual will be uncomfortable or unwilling to take special measures to address an opportunity in case something goes wrong.

Risk-seeking individuals, however, are prone to the opposite polarities of response preferences. Threats are likely to be accepted or ignored, with the attitude that they are part of normal life and can be addressed without special action. Indeed the need to respond proactively to a threat may even be seen as a sign of weakness by the risk-seeker, who takes pride in the ability to cope with emergent risks or problems. Contingency may be considered for serious threats, but the risk-seeker is more likely to rely on reactive action taken if/when the threat turns into a real problem. Risk transfer of threats will be seen as the last refuge of the inadequate, admitting that the challenge of a particular threat is too difficult. The risk-seeking response to opportunity is often to be overconfident, choosing inappropriately aggressive response strategies in an attempt to capture additional benefits.

IMPLEMENTATION

The Implementation stage involves taking planned actions and monitoring their effectiveness. It is at this point in the risk management process that many organizations fail to reap the rewards of the preceding stages. Identification, Assessment and Response Planning are merely gathering information about the various risks faced by the project or the business, analyzing its significance and determining options for action. But it is only when those actions are actually implemented that risk exposure is changed, by minimizing or removing threats, and by maximizing or capturing opportunities.

The degree of commitment shown by individuals during the Implementation phase is driven by their risk attitude, with risk-averse people tending to be very conscientious in completing agreed responses, and pressing for immediate action. Their sensitivity to the presence of uncertainty drives them to take whatever measures are necessary to reduce risk exposure, and indeed they may even go beyond the scope of agreed actions, gold-plating the response 'just in case'. Risk-seeking people by contrast are more likely to lack commitment to implementation of proactive risk responses, taking short-cuts where possible, preferring to 'take their chances and see what happens', confident in their ability to deal with whatever occurs, and relishing the challenge of beating the odds.

Similar discrepancies are likely to occur when reporting risk results. A risk-averse person will emphasize the presence of threats and play down possible opportunities, while focusing on the need for proactive action. A risk report describing the same situation but written by a risk-seeking person will downplay any negative implications of uncertainty and is more likely to state that everything is proceeding according to plan, with significant opportunities for improvement.

PROCESS MANAGEMENT

The final phase in the risk management process is to review and update all information in order to ensure that the current position is reflected. The changing nature of risk requires the risk process to be cyclic, regularly reviewing risk exposure, identifying and assessing new risks, and ensuring appropriate responses. As for previous phases, the degree of commitment shown to keeping the risk management process alive and current will vary according to the risk attitude of the individual concerned, with risk-aversion increasing commitment and risk-seeking reducing it.

RISK MANAGEMENT AND THE GROUP

Consideration of the effect of the risk attitudes of individuals on the risk management process can form a basis for looking at group influences, since groups are made up from individuals. It is, however, important to remember that the characteristics of groups are not merely the sum or the average of their component parts. This is true for risk attitudes in group settings: although individual risk attitudes are significant influences on the approach taken by the group to uncertainty, there are other factors involved which create a corporate perspective.

Groups operate at a number of levels, both formal and informal, including:

- project teams
- peer groups
- technical specialist communities

- functional departments

- the organization

- friends and colleagues

- social groups within the work context

- societal groups outside work.

To consider each of these groups separately is beyond the scope of this book, and would introduce a confusing level of granularity to the discussion without shedding significant additional light on the underlying influences. It is, however, important in the context of understanding and managing risk attitudes to distinguish between the small *working team* and the overall *organization*, since these are the two primary groups which tend to exert a significant influence over risk-based decisions in the workplace. It is necessary to understand why and how the approach to risk displayed by groups at the working team and overall organizational levels can modify the effectiveness of the risk management process both for projects and for the business. Once this is understood, steps can be taken to address the group influence in order to enhance risk management effectiveness.

WORKING TEAM INFLUENCES

The working team is taken here to mean the smallest functional unit responsible for completing a defined task. Most commonly this will be a project team, constituted for the life of a particular project and mandated to achieve a specified scope and objectives.

The discussion above on the influence of individual risk attitudes on the risk management process might suggest the possibility of building 'risk-balanced teams' containing representatives across the range of possible risk attitudes. This concept would seem to be a natural extension of well-established work on teamwork which recommends that other aspects of personality should be assessed and considered when constructing a new working team. Frameworks such as the Myers-Briggs Type Indicator, Belbin Team Roles and the Margerison-McCann Team Management Wheel illustrate the value of such an approach. However, although some of these existing frameworks include assessment of some elements of risk attitude, the idea of the risk-balanced team is quite different.

Building such a team would require each individual to adopt a consistent risk attitude in all situations, so that their position on the risk attitude spectrum could be reliably characterized. But the particular risk attitude of a given individual can vary according to a number of criteria (as discussed in Chapter 4). The same person might be risk-averse in one situation and risk-seeking in another. Risk attitude is situational, even though individuals may have habituated a particular default attitude which acts as their starting point in most situations. Consequently it is not possible to build a risk-balanced team of different risk attitudes in the same way as can be done for personality types.

Nevertheless the same result can be obtained in a different way. If the aim is for a working team to have the optimum balance of risk attitudes shared between its members, and if each person can choose an appropriate risk attitude, then the necessary balance is achievable. It requires each individual in the working team to be sufficiently self-aware of their risk attitude, and also for them to be able to modify their attitudes towards risk where needed. In this case the team becomes automatically and organically 'risk-balanced', with members adopting appropriate positions in response to the current situation and the needs of the team.

The value of such a risk-balanced team is self-evident. Clearly a working team where all the members shared the same prevailing risk attitude would suffer from the same issues that affect individuals, as outlined in the preceding section. In fact a homogeneous team would exhibit enhanced biases since the influences of team members would reinforce one another, leading to even more extreme effects on the effectiveness of the risk management process. A wholly risk-averse team might never take any risks, becoming paralyzed with fear in case any threats materialized. Similarly a working team comprising all risk-seekers might take unnecessary risks that jeopardize project or organizational wellbeing, encouraging one another to ever more daring feats of bravado.

If it were possible to build a risk-balanced team where individual preferences were identified and understood (without blame or criticism), then instead of the negative aspects of each risk attitude type prevailing, the team could reach a position of synergy, where the strengths of one risk attitude complement the strengths of others. In such a team the risk-seeking individuals would encourage the team to step out of the comfort zone, to be prepared to reach for opportunities and challenge threats, and to accept that a degree of risk-taking is required in order to achieve any objectives that are worth achieving. Their natural inbuilt optimism would be tempered by the caution of their risk-averse colleagues, who would be able to play devil's advocate and point out potential pitfalls, avoiding unnecessary risks without becoming overly pessimistic.

The set of skills required for such self-awareness and sensitivity to the attitudes of others comes under the heading of 'emotional literacy', and is the subject of Part 3 of this book. Here it is enough to say that a successful risk-balanced working team must have a high degree of emotional literacy.

ORGANIZATIONAL INFLUENCES

The second level of group where risk attitudes exert an influence is the overall organization. Like a working team, the organization itself possesses and displays a corporate risk attitude. However, whereas the approach to risk of a working team is largely a function of the risk attitudes of the constituent individuals, an organization is different. Each organization can be said to have its own distinct 'corporate risk culture' which influences every action and decision, often covertly, and which is more than the sum of its component parts.

While the area of individual risk attitudes has been well characterized and understood, parallel issues relating to corporate risk culture are less well recognized. Indeed it is often not readily accepted that an organization can have a distinctly defined approach to uncertainty, in a similar way that individuals hold risk attitudes. This is partly driven by the wider discussion over whether an organization as an entity can have a 'company culture' or display 'organizational psychology' or 'corporate behaviour'. One useful working definition of culture is 'the shared beliefs, values and knowledge of a group of people with a common purpose'. Clearly this definition can be applied to the approach adopted by a given organization towards risk, whether this forms part of a broader culture or not. And the natural expression of such shared beliefs, values and knowledge is found in the attitudes displayed by the organization. In the context of this book, these can be termed 'corporate or organizational risk attitudes'.

The drivers of corporate risk culture are many and varied, and include:

- the influence of organizational history and corporate memory
- recent events having a significant effect on the organization
- reputational issues, past and present
- stakeholder expectations and influences
- the leadership style adopted at all levels in the organization
- characteristics of the industry sector within which the organization operates
- the current economic environment and conditions
- the national and international context for corporate activities.

Each of these factors exerts a significant influence over the organization's approach to uncertainty, which in turn has an effect on the way projects and the business are run.

A number of strategic decisions are made by organizations which have a direct

Table 2.3 Influence of organizational risk attitudes on strategic decisions

Strategic decision	Influence of risk-aversion	Influence of risk-seeking
Set risk thresholds	Set low risk thresholds. Reduce thresholds further in response to stakeholder concerns.	Set high risk thresholds. Resist pressure from stakeholders to modify thresholds.
Determine contingency levels	Set high contingency levels, tending to over-provide, reducing funds available for other purposes. Tend to allocate contingency too readily in in response to variations from plan.	Set low contingency levels, tending to under-provide, limiting ability to respond to risks which occur. View contingency as additional profit, to be retained not spent.
Set financial objectives	Set low targets that fail to stretch the organization.	Set high targets that may be unachievable.
Attitude to staff risk-taking	Penalize staff for taking risks as this is viewed as irresponsible.	Penalize staff for spending time on the risk process as this is viewed as unnecessary.
Investment strategy	Cautious, leading to loss of opportunity and failure to capture potential additional benefits.	Overconfident, taking on high risks without clear benefits.
Portfolio management	Preference for low-risk/low-return projects.	Preference for high-risk/high-return projects.
Strategic positioning	Maintain the status quo. Avoid innovation.	Adopt responsive stance. Encourage innovation.
Resourcing for risk management	Over-invest in risk management. Conscientious implementation of proactive risk responses.	Under-invest in risk management. Spend resources on fire-fighting and crisis management.

effect on the management of risk in specific projects and more generally in the business. Each is an expression of corporate risk culture, and as such it will vary according to organizational risk attitude. Similar shorthand phrases can be used to describe the polarities of organizational risk attitude as were used above for individuals, namely 'risk-averse' and 'risk-seeking'. These attitudes result in different outcomes and behaviours in a number of key areas which have a direct effect on risk management effectiveness, as discussed below (and summarized in Table 2.3):

- *Setting risk thresholds.* Every organization has to decide the degree of risk which it is prepared to take, both for the business as a whole and for its operations, programmes and projects. This is known as the 'risk threshold', and it may be expressed in various ways at different levels of the organization. But senior management cannot simply decide their risk threshold in isolation; they must also take account of the views of a wide range of stakeholders at all levels of the business, each of whom has different interests and concerns.

  Some stakeholders are individuals, others are groups of various sizes; some are internal to the organization while others are external; some are independent while others are connected and influenced by each other. Stakeholders have different interests in different levels of the organization, with some being concerned for the overall business while others are only interested in individual projects. The degree of influence stakeholders can exercise over the business or its projects also differs widely.

  The web of interleaving interests and influences is necessarily very complex, but it is made more so by the fact that each stakeholder (whether individual or group) also possesses a particular attitude to risk, as well as their own risk threshold. These will influence the overall risk attitude of the organization, either directly or in more subtle ways, leading to modifications of the risk threshold set by corporate management. The risk-averse organization is likely to set low risk thresholds and reduce them further in response to stakeholder influence, whereas the risk-seeking organization will prefer higher thresholds and will resist any outside influence to modify them.

- *Determining contingency levels.* Senior management must set the corporate policy for contingency, including the level of additional resources to be set aside to respond to emergent risk (both threats and opportunities), as well as the subsequent contingency management process. Contingency may be divided into various elements to be managed by different parts of the organization, from 'management reserve' for senior management, to 'project contingency' for which the project manager is responsible.

One key area of contingency management which is significantly influenced by corporate risk culture is the attitude taken towards contingency funds. If risk management is seen as an unwelcome overhead or a bureaucratic necessity, and if there is no genuine commitment to its proactive use, contingency funds can be regarded as 'hidden profit' to be taken back at any time. A more mature attitude to risk would recognize that contingency exists to be spent in order to avoid or minimize threats and to exploit or maximize opportunities so that achievement of objectives is optimized.

A risk-averse organization might be expected to over-provide in its contingency fund, sequestering resources that might otherwise be available for investment or additional projects. A risk-seeking organization conversely might under-provide, limiting the ability to respond when threats or opportunities materialize which require additional resources.

- *Other financial objectives.* Organizations set a variety of financial targets for the business and operational elements, including margin, profit, return on investment (ROI), internal rate of return (IRR) and so on. Similar to contingency funding, the levels at which these targets are set is determined by corporate risk attitude. Risk-aversion might result in lower targets that fail to stretch the organization, but which are easier and less risky to achieve. Targets set by risk-seeking organizations or management teams are likely to be more challenging.

- *Approach to risk-taking.* Closely linked to the setting of financial targets is the way the organization views risk-taking by employees at all levels. If risk is welcomed as a natural consequence of being in business, and the need to take sensible risks in order to reap benefits is recognized, then the organization should be prepared to reward those members of staff who take risks appropriately. This is true from senior managers to shop-floor workers, where the risk-mature organization will view risk-taking as good practice as long as it is in the context of effective risk management. Organizations whose approach to risk management is less mature will not be so enlightened, and will tend to penalize staff for taking risks or spending time on the risk management process, either because they are perceived as acting irresponsibly (the viewpoint of the risk-averse organization), or because they are seen as wasting time on a needless process (the risk-seeking perspective). The consequence of these attitudes to risk-taking is to discourage expenditure of effort on risk management, with inevitable implications for project and business performance.

- *Investment strategy.* The strategy for growth and development adopted by the organization will be driven by the corporate risk culture, as a special case of the effect on risk-taking. This is particularly likely to influence investment strategy, including the approach to mergers and acquisitions, since the organization may either be prepared to take on such business risks even if the benefits are not clear or guaranteed (risk-seeking), or may be overly cautious (risk-averse) and lose the benefits.

- *Portfolio management.* The organization's approach to its overall risk profile is also affected by the corporate risk culture. The aim should be to produce a 'risk-balanced portfolio', containing a number of low-risk investments and projects where a lower return might also be expected, balanced with some high-risk/high-return initiatives, as well as some 'business as usual' work. Risk-aversion is likely to tip the balance towards the low-risk elements of the mix, whereas risk-seeking will encourage the organization to take on more high-risk ventures.

- *Strategic positioning (marketing and product development).* Another area influenced by the risk attitude of the organization is the strategic positioning of the business within its chosen market, together with the ambitions and targets set for the future. Organizations less comfortable with uncertainty will tend to maintain the status quo and be less innovative, running the risk of stagnation and decline. Those with a proclivity towards taking risks will be more fluid and responsive to the marketplace, though they may fail to consolidate gains, and may also over-reach themselves by taking on too much risk. Similar arguments apply to the new product development or innovation strategy.

- *Resourcing risk management.* The final area influenced by the organizational attitude to risk is the amount of resource made available for risk management, both in terms of funding the risk process and also in committing additional resources to implementation of agreed risk responses. In risk-seeking organizations where the risk process is seen as an unnecessary burden preventing creativity and restricting the ability of the business to react, under-investment is common. This produces a vicious circle where lack of investment in risk management resources leads to failure to manage risks effectively, and threats materialize into problems while opportunities are missed. The risk-seeking organization therefore has to spend more time fire-fighting in crisis management mode. They can end up spending more on recovery than was saved by not implementing the risk process, leaving less resources available to invest in risk management in future. This cycle is illustrated in the left-hand loop of Figure 2.2.

By contrast, risk-averse organizations who are nervous about risk are more likely to over-invest in risk management, and may introduce a restrictive framework that hinders execution of normal business. Here the risk process can become such a burden that it ceases to be effective, with the

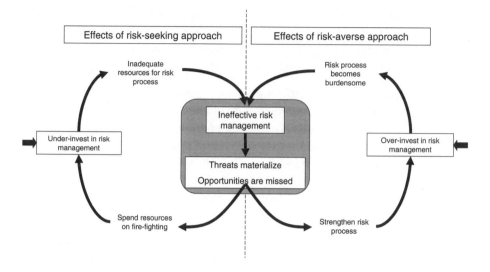

Figure 2.2   Effect of corporate risk attitude on risk management resourcing

same result that threats occur and opportunities are lost. Again a self-fulfilling prophecy occurs, where the fears of the risk-averse organization become reality as a direct result of their over-burdensome risk process, leading them to introduce even more rigorous risk procedures which worsen the effect (see the right-hand side of Figure 2.2).

It is interesting to note from Figure 2.2 that both risk-averse and risk-seeking organizational attitudes are likely to affect risk management effectiveness adversely, emphasizing the importance of understanding and managing risk attitude at corporate level as well as for individuals.

DIAGNOSIS IS NOT THE SAME AS TREATMENT

The discussion in this chapter has demonstrated that the approach to uncertainty and risk adopted and displayed by individuals and groups exerts a significant influence over the effectiveness of the risk management process for both projects and the business. There is no doubt that these 'soft factors' have a concrete impact.

However, it is also true that this whole area is generally not well understood and therefore not well managed in business. Human factors are often seen as the realm of the personnel department, who deal primarily with staff issues such as recruitment, training and development. There seems to be no natural home in the organization to take responsibility for understanding and managing the risk attitudes of individuals, teams or the organization itself.

This is largely the reason why risk management fails to deliver the expected benefits to projects and businesses. Chapter 1 demonstrated that risk management matters, as it offers a framework for proactively addressing the effects of uncertainty on achievement of objectives. This chapter has listed a range of Critical Success Factors (see Table 2.1), and asserted that the most important is the human element, since it exerts influence at both individual and group levels over the effectiveness of risk management across the organization.

If risk management is important but not performing, and if human factors are the most influential CSF over risk management effectiveness, there is a clear need to understand and manage these soft aspects, at both individual and corporate levels. Unfortunately there is currently no structured way to do this. Traditional approaches to risk management rely mainly on implementation of a methodology, with suitable process support from the 'Three Ts' (tools, techniques and training). However, risk management is likely to continue to fail until organizations find a way of dealing with the soft side.

Given that understanding is an indispensable precursor to management, it is now necessary to consider in detail how risk attitudes arise, and what influences them. This can be addressed at individual and group levels, and these are covered in Part 2. Having understood the issues to be tackled, it is then possible to consider candidate approaches for managing these risk attitudes proactively and effectively, drawing on the field of emotional literacy as described in Part 3. Finally understanding can be translated into action as shown in Part 4, which reaches towards the ultimate goal of effective management of risk attitudes.

Understanding Risk Attitudes

CHAPTER 3

General Principles of Risk Attitudes

Since human factors in general, and risk attitudes in particular, have such a significant influence over the risk management process at both individual and group levels, as discussed in Chapter 2, they clearly require proactive management if the risk process is to be optimally effective. However, the first step to being able to manage something is to understand it. This chapter therefore addresses the general topic of risk attitudes, with particular influences over risk attitudes being covered in the following chapters.

In Chapter 1 'risk' was defined as 'an uncertainty that could have a positive or negative effect on one or more objectives', and 'attitude' was defined as 'chosen state of mind, mental view or disposition with regard to a fact or state'. Combining the two gives a working definition of 'risk attitude' as 'a chosen state of mind with regard to those uncertainties that could have a positive or negative effect on objectives, driven by perception', or more simply 'a chosen response to perception of uncertainty that matters'. An individual's view of risk is driven by perception ('How uncertain? And how much does it matter to objectives?'), and so is their attitude ('How do I view this fact or situation?'). As a result, the definition of risk attitude needs to take account of perception. A more complete definition of risk attitude would therefore be '**chosen response to uncertainty that matters, driven by perception**'. Since perception is inherently subjective, it naturally follows that the risk attitude of a particular person or group towards a given uncertain situation might be different from the attitude adopted by others.

The discussion of risk attitudes in this chapter covers both individuals and groups, based on the principle outlined in Chapter 2 that the attitudes of groups are largely (though not exclusively) influenced by the constituent individuals. The factors affecting the risk attitudes of individuals and groups are then covered in more detail in later chapters.

THE RISK ATTITUDE SPECTRUM

A range of possible *attitudes* can be adopted towards the same situation, and these result in differing *behaviours*, which lead to *consequences*, both intended and unintended, as illustrated in Figure 3.1. Indeed behaviour is the only reliable diagnostic indicator of inner attitude, and considerable attention has therefore been

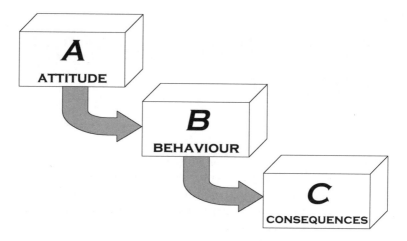

Figure 3.1   Attitude, behaviour and consequences

paid to behavioural psychology and management by those seeking to understand and manage the effects of human factors in business. Another approach, however, which might prove more fruitful, is to seek to understand and address the underlying attitudes, rather than concentrating on the presenting behavioural symptoms.

Although attitude manifests itself through behaviour, there are other drivers of behaviour which can displace the chosen or preferred attitude. The extent to which this occurs depends on the perception of the situation towards which the attitude is being directed. This is best understood by considering the two extremes, where the situation is perceived as good or neutral, and where it is seen as bad:

- *Favourable or neutral situation.* When a situation or environment is perceived as positive or benign, behaviour is driven largely by attitude (Figure 3.2). In this case the attitudinal choice of the individual or group is the key determinant of behaviour. For example when faced with an existing client who is open to the possibility of taking on new business, an organization may decide to pursue the opportunity or to ignore it ('take it or leave it'). This choice is not mandated by the situation, and the organization is free to select its preferred response. People who adopt this attitude consistently may be labelled as optimists, since they tend to view all situations as equally positive. This helps them to retain control of their behaviour since the key driver when the environment is positive is the chosen attitude, allowing a proactive response to the prevailing situation.

- *Unfavourable or hostile situation.* When an individual or group perceives a situation or environment as negative, the resulting behaviour is largely determined by a direct response to the situation, and attitude plays a smaller role. This is illustrated in Figure 3.3. For example in a setting where one's

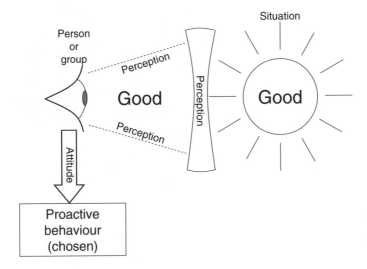

Figure 3.2   Behaviour in neutral or positive environments

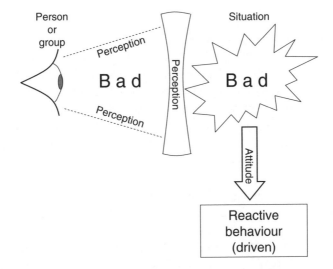

Figure 3.3   Behaviour in hostile environments

personal safety is threatened, the 'fight or flight or freeze' response is adopted almost unthinkingly, regardless of the prevailing attitude of the individual. Indeed a negative situation may force behaviour which is contrary to that preferred by attitude, leading to a more reactive stance. Individuals who regularly adopt reactive behaviour driven by a perception that the environment is negative may be termed pessimists, and in extreme cases this may even lead to paranoia.

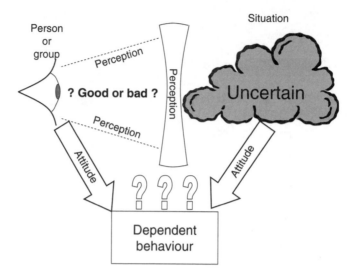

Figure 3.4   Behaviour in uncertain environments

Although the responses to positive and negative situations suggest at first sight that environment or situation is the prime determinant of behaviour, in fact it is how the environment is *perceived* by each person, since a situation that appears hostile to one may seem benign to another. This raises the question of what influences behaviour when the situation is *uncertain*. In this case the important driver of behaviour is whether uncertainty is perceived as favourable, neutral, unfavourable or hostile (Figure 3.4). This reaction to uncertainty is 'risk attitude', defined above as 'chosen response to perception of significant uncertainty'.

Risk attitudes have been studied by a range of academic and organizational researchers in recent years, and there is a considerable and growing body of knowledge and evidence in this area. Much of this has been obtained by studying behaviour in games of chance, financial investments, gamblers (including lottery players) and people betting on sports (especially horse racing). Given the practical focus of this book and the aim of understanding in order to manage, such research is not detailed or repeated here. The discussion that follows however draws on this body of knowledge, and is fully consistent with its findings.

One key conclusion on which researchers and practitioners are agreed is that risk attitudes exist on a spectrum. The same uncertain situation will elicit different preferred attitudes from different individuals or groups, depending on how they perceive the uncertainty. And since attitude drives behaviour, different people will exhibit different responses to the same situation, as a result of their differing underlying risk attitudes (sometimes called 'perceptual dissonance') – a situation regarded as too risky by one person will be seen as acceptable by another.

There are, however, a number of other situations which might cause the position on the risk attitude spectrum to vary, in addition to the natural variation in perception between individuals and groups. As the degree or intensity of uncertainty changes (either in reality or through changed perception), the strength of reaction of a given individual or group also changes. And there are a range of influences both internal and external which can move an individual or a group from one position on the spectrum to another. These are considered below, after first addressing the basic alternative positions on the risk attitude spectrum.

BASIC RISK ATTITUDES

The variety of possible responses to a given level of risk is illustrated by the curve in Figure 3.5. The precise shape of the curve is not significant for this discussion, but its general characteristics expose some important aspects of the range of risk attitudes displayed by individuals and groups when faced with uncertainty. The curve has two halves, representing those individuals and groups who are uncomfortable with uncertainty (lower-left) and those who are comfortable (upper-right). There is a flat section in the centre where individuals or groups are more or less indifferent about the

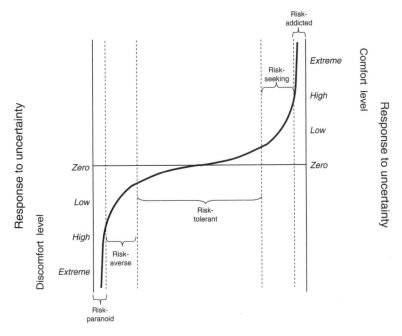

Figure 3.5   Spectrum of risk attitudes

given level of uncertainty, but the response becomes more extreme (either comfort or discomfort) towards the ends of the spectrum.

Given this basic shape, it is possible to distinguish a number of key regions on the curve, and to use labels of convenience to describe each area. The term 'risk-averse' is used for those who regard risk as unwelcome and to be feared and avoided. Those who see risk as a challenge to be overcome are called 'risk-seeking'. There are clearly more extreme positions which might be called 'risk-paranoid' (paralyzed by any form of uncertainty) and 'risk-addicted' (an unhealthy preoccupation with uncertainty), but these are not common and probably represent attitudes and resultant behaviours requiring corrective intervention. Between the two usual polarities of risk-averse and risk-seeking are two other common positions. A 'risk-tolerant' person or group has an attitude which is ambivalent or accepting of risk, viewing it as a normal part of life. 'Risk-neutral' on the other hand (not shown in Figure 3.5) is neither risk-averse nor risk-seeking, describing a person or group tending to view risk impartially in the short-term, but prepared to take risk if there is a significant long-term benefit.

The four basic risk attitudes are well understood and can be clearly defined, as follows:

- A *risk-averse* person or group feels uncomfortable with uncertainty, has a low tolerance for ambiguity, and seeks security and resolution in the face of risk. People who are risk-averse tend to be practical, accepting and have common sense, enjoying facts more than theories and supporting established methods of working. When applied to threats this attitude is likely to lead to increased sensitivity and over-reaction, as the presence of a threat causes discomfort to people with a risk-averse attitude. This has a significant effect on all aspects of the risk process, as threats are perceived more readily by the risk-averse and are assessed as more severe, leading to a preference for aggressive risk responses to avoid or minimize as many threats as possible. When applied to opportunities, however, a risk-averse attitude is likely to lead to the opposite result, as the person or group may not see as many opportunities, or may tend to underrate their significance, and may not be prepared to take the steps necessary to enhance or capture the opportunity. As a result, risk-aversion tends to over-react to threats and under-react to opportunities.

- *Risk-tolerance* implies being reasonably comfortable with most uncertainty, accepting that it exists as a normal feature of everyday life, including projects and business. The risk-tolerant person or group tends to take uncertainty in their stride, with no apparent or significant influence on their behaviour. For both threats and opportunities this may lead to a failure to appreciate the importance of the potential effect of the risk on achievement of objectives, whether the impact is upside or downside, as the laissez-faire approach fails to result in proactive action. This may be the most dangerous of all the risk attitudes, since the acceptance of risk as part of the 'normal situation' may mean it is not managed appropriately, leading to more problems from impacted threats, and loss of potential benefits as a result of missed opportunities. Risk-tolerance may appear balanced, but progress cannot be made while remaining perfectly balanced.

- A *risk-neutral* attitude sees present risk-taking as a price worth paying for future pay-offs. Risk-neutral individuals and groups are neither risk-averse nor risk-seeking, but rather seek strategies and tactics that have high future pay-offs. They think abstractly and creatively and envisage possibilities, enjoying ideas and not being afraid of change or the unknown. For both threats and opportunities this risk-neutral approach is quite mature, focusing on the longer term and only taking action when it is likely to lead to significant benefit.

- People and groups who are *risk-seeking* tend to be adaptable and resourceful, enjoying life and not afraid to take action. This can lead to a somewhat casual approach towards threats, as the risk-seeker welcomes the challenge of tackling the uncertainty head-on, pitching their skills and abilities against the vagaries of fate. The thrill of the chase can outweigh the potential for harm, leading to unwise decisions and actions. During the risk process the risk-seeking person or group is likely to identify fewer threats as they see these as part of normal business. Any threats that are raised are likely to be underestimated both in probability and possible impact, and acceptance will be the preferred response. The effect of risk-seeking on opportunities is quite different, however. Risk-seekers will be sensitive to possible opportunities, may overestimate their importance and will wish to pursue them aggressively.

It is important to note from Figure 3.5 that risk attitudes are not discrete, but occupy a continuous spectrum with no clear boundaries between the various headline attitudes. It is therefore possible for a particular individual or group to be 'highly risk-averse' without being risk-paranoid, or 'slightly risk-seeking' without being risk-tolerant. It is also true that the same individual or group may exhibit different risk attitudes under different circumstances. It is therefore a mistake to think that every person or group can be unambiguously labelled with a single risk attitude, although the four common terms represent real and distinct typical states. Most people and groups appear to be habituated to a single preferred risk attitude which might represent their natural first response to uncertainty (unless they are sufficiently aware and emotionally literate to be able to modify this), but this starting point can be influenced by a number of factors, as discussed below and in later chapters.

SITUATIONAL INFLUENCES ON PREFERRED RISK ATTITUDE

Individual risk attitudes tend to be driven by subconscious preferences developed in a person over a long period of time, partly as a result of personal upbringing and partly in response to previous experiences. Similarly groups exhibit a preferred risk attitude based on their past history.

However, the current environment in which individuals and groups find themselves also has a significant effect on the way uncertainty is perceived. There are a large number of situational factors which can modify the preferred risk attitude. These typically act by influencing whether a particular situation is perceived as uncertain or not, and the preferred attitude (and resulting behaviour) is then driven by whether that uncertainty is perceived as welcome or unwelcome.

These situational factors include the following:

- *Level of relevant skills, knowledge or expertise.* Where an individual or group is confronting an uncertain situation of which they have no prior knowledge or experience, the tendency is to perceive the situation as more risky, leading to a more risk-averse reaction. If, however, the situation exists in a domain where the individual or group have proven skills or expertise, the degree of risk is played down and a more risk-seeking response may be adopted. Both of these situations may result in unrealistic or inappropriate assessments of the level of risk, with undue weight being given to the presence or absence of relevant skills, knowledge or expertise.

- *Perception of probability or frequency of occurrence.* If the risk under consideration is believed to be unlikely to occur, the preferred risk attitude tends to shift towards the risk-seeking end of the spectrum. Higher perceived probability leads to increased risk-aversion. This perception may be held in contradiction to the existence of data demonstrating actual frequency.

- *Perception of impact magnitude, either severity of negative threats or size of positive opportunities.* As for risk probability, perception of possible impact should the risk occur can influence risk attitude. If the risk is a threat with a high perceived negative impact, risk attitude becomes more risk-averse. Likewise a higher degree of risk-seeking is encouraged by opportunities whose potential benefits are perceived as significant and also by threats whose possible adverse effects are seen as small.

- *Degree of perceived control or choice in the situation.* Manageability is a key factor in assessment of risk, and will influence the preferred risk attitude. Where the extent to which an individual or group is able to affect a risk is perceived as low, either proactively in advance or reactively should the risk occur, a more risk-averse attitude tends to be taken. If manageability is seen as high, risk-seeking is encouraged.

- *Closeness of the risk in time.* Uncertain events that could occur in the near future ('temporal proximity') are perceived as more risky than those further away, even if an objective assessment of probability, impact and manageability suggests otherwise.

- *Potential for direct consequences.* Uncertain events that could have a direct effect on the individual or the group are also perceived as more important than those which affect others. (For individuals this factor is sometimes termed 'personal propinquity'.)

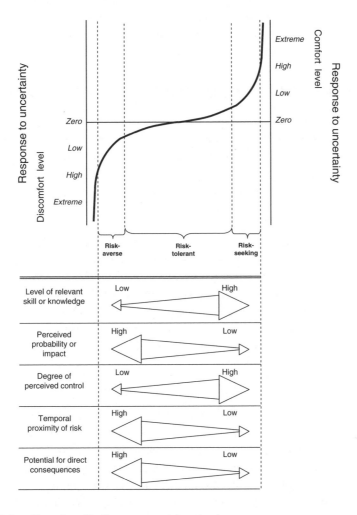

Figure 3.6   Situational influences on risk attitude

The effect of these situational factors on preferred risk attitude are illustrated in Figure 3.6.

The existence of these factors creates a situational aspect to risk attitude. The same individual or group may exhibit different risk attitudes in different situations. For example an individual may be conservative in their approach to work or career (risk-averse) but may undertake freefall paragliding as a recreational hobby (risk-seeking). This difference in chosen or preferred risk attitude is driven not by some innate generic characteristic, but by situational perceptions. Perhaps this individual may consider that their job is under threat as a result of a corporate reorganization or market changes, so they feel reluctant to take unnecessary risks with their career. However, when relaxing outside work they may feel the need to compensate for the restrictions of their employment situation by engaging in a risky pastime which they do not see as a threat since they have been doing it for some time.

INTERNAL INFLUENCES ON PREFERRED RISK ATTITUDE

The situational influencers of risk attitude described above mainly arise from the perception of the external environment. There is, however, an internal environment which has an equally profound effect on the way uncertainty is perceived, and hence is able to influence the preferred risk attitude of an individual or a group. These underlying psychological influences which affect attitudes towards uncertainty are known as *heuristics*.

A heuristic is defined as 'an approach to inferring a solution to a problem by reasoning from previous experience, when no relevant algorithm or dataset exists'. The term is derived from the Greek word *heuriskein*, meaning to discover, implying an attempt to make sense of a new situation by referring to what already exists. Heuristics offer a proven approach to problem-solving and learning, with widespread applications in mathematics and science, and the heuristic approach is also used as a teaching method where pupils are encouraged to learn for themselves through guided experiment, investigation and discovery.

In the context of risk attitudes, heuristics describe attempts by an individual or group to analyse an uncertain situation and determine the appropriate response by referring to some previous experience. This often occurs subconsciously as an integral part of the assessment of risk, leading to sources of bias when considering a situation where the answer is unknown or unfamiliar, and where a person is required to make a judgement with insufficient information. Of course if the operation of a particular heuristic is identified it can be countered and adjusted for, since all heuristics function in a systematic manner.

CONCLUSION AND SUMMARY

This chapter has introduced the concept of the risk attitude as a chosen response to uncertainty, driven by whether that uncertainty is perceived as positive or negative. A range of possible attitudes are possible, from risk-averse through risk-tolerant to risk-seeking, each of which carries implications for the approach to risk management adopted by the individual or group. Each individual and group has a preferred or default attitude to risk, arising from their previous experience and past history. There are also however many situational influences with the ability to modify the preferred risk attitude of an individual or a group, including internal and external factors.

Issues present in the external environment are relatively simple to identify, and their influence over risk attitudes is usually fairly explicit. As a result it is usually quite straightforward to compensate for them. Internal heuristics are, however, more difficult to identify and manage since they arise in the personal or collective subconscious. The next two chapters therefore concentrate on these factors, with the most typical heuristics influencing individual risk attitudes discussed in Chapter 4 and group heuristics covered in Chapter 5.

Individual Risk Attitudes and Heuristics

Previous chapters have developed an understanding of risk attitudes as chosen responses to uncertain situations, driven by whether uncertainty is perceived as favourable, neutral or hostile. A range of possible risk attitudes exists, from risk-averse to risk-seeking, reflecting the preferred response to a given level of perceived uncertainty. The same principles apply equally to individuals and to groups, with a range of possible responses determined by perception of uncertainty.

It is important to realize that risk attitudes are driven by perceptions, which may not necessarily reflect reality. For both individuals and groups, there are many factors which influence how uncertainty is perceived. Some of these factors are overt and visible, while others are covert and hidden. However, although groups are made up of individuals, the factors affecting individual risk attitudes are different from those influencing groups.

Overt influences are more readily managed since they are straightforward to identify. It is more difficult however to deal with the covert factors influencing risk attitude. This chapter addresses a range of such influences which can operate on individuals facing uncertainty, with group influences covered in the following chapter. This allows a bottom-up approach, considering first those 'internal' influences arising from within individuals, then addressing how these might be modified by group, organizational or national contexts. Of course there are also group-specific factors which are not simply the aggregate of influences over the individual comprising the group, and these are also discussed in Chapter 5.

COVERT FACTORS INFLUENCING INDIVIDUAL RISK ATTITUDE

Attitudes towards uncertainty are affected significantly by underlying psychological influences known as *heuristics*, as discussed in the previous chapter. Many of these influences were first described in the context of decision-making by Amos Tversky, Daniel Kahneman, Paul Slovic and their collaborators in the 1960s to 1980s, and their seminal work is not reproduced here since our interest is specifically in the effect of heuristics on risk attitudes.

Heuristics can subconsciously and systematically introduce sources of bias when considering a situation where the answer is unknown or unfamiliar, and where a person is required to make a judgement with insufficient information. Their operation can be recognized by the use of several alternative terms, such as 'rule-of-thumb', 'gut feel' or 'intuition'. These common names indicate that heuristics do not operate in the conscious realm, but are covert influences on thinking and decision-making processes. They also suggest that heuristics are used to simplify decision-making by providing a short-cut which produces an answer without the need for rigorous analysis or calculation. Each heuristic results in consideration of only a subset of available data in order to reach a judgement on the degree of uncertainty present in a given situation.

While this could be seen as a more efficient way of assessing uncertainty, it also results in a number of biases due to the subconscious nature of the influence of heuristics. When the operation of a heuristic is hidden its effects cannot be managed. If, however, the presence of a particular heuristic is identified, it can be countered and adjusted for, since all heuristics function in a systematic manner.

Behavioural psychologists have identified a large number of heuristics which operate at the subconscious level, but not all act directly on risk attitudes. The most typical heuristics influencing individual risk attitudes are:

- *availability* – more memorable events are treated as more significant;

- *representativeness* – using similarity to stereotypes as an indicator of significance;

- *anchoring and adjustment* – starting from an initial estimate and varying around it, even if the initial value has no objective basis in fact;

- *confirmation trap* – seeking and weighting evidence which substantiates a prior conviction, and ignoring contrary data.

Other heuristics operate at the organizational and group level and these are discussed in Chapter 5.

It is important to understand these factors capable of influencing individual risk attitudes, so that their effect can be countered and managed proactively where they lead to inappropriate responses to uncertainty.

The following sections discuss each of the major individual heuristics in turn: defining the source of bias, describing how it influences risk attitude, providing examples and outlining its relevance to risk process. Part 4 of this book presents strategies for using the insights and approaches of emotional literacy to diagnose and address these heuristics.

THE AVAILABILITY HEURISTIC

> Imagine a school classroom where the teacher has just asked the children a question. A large and loud child in the front row immediately puts up his hand and waves it enthusiastically, saying 'Oooh, oooh, I know, me, me, pick me...', while all the other children sit quietly behind him. Which child will the teacher tend to choose to give an answer?

When considering how to respond to an uncertain situation which has not previously been encountered, the human brain performs a subconscious search for relevant data to use as a basis against which to compare the present situation. Memories are rapidly accessed in an attempt to find something to use as a reference point. Of course a great deal of data resides in each person's memory, so some filtering process is required in order to determine which information is relevant. One of the main subconscious filtering processes is the *availability heuristic*. The basic principle in operation here is that if a particular data item is easier to recall than others, then its relevance is assumed to be higher. The primary driver is the extent to which the data item is *available* to the memory.

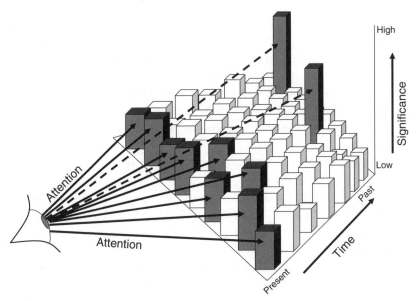

Figure 4.1   The availability heuristic

While this seems sensible at first, there are several factors which influence the ease with which a particular data item can be recalled. In particular, items which are *more recent* tend to be easier to recall than those which are more distant in time, and *more dramatic* items are more memorable than those which are closer to the average. Figure 4.1 illustrates this effect, with attention drawn to recent events, as well as to two dramatic events in the past, but ignoring the bulk of average data.

The way in which a past event can be assessed as dramatic is also important here. Clearly some events are significant because of their high impact on objectives (for example particularly costly, very late or unusually good reputational impact). But it is also possible for past events to be more available to the memory if they have higher emotional content; that is, they matter more to the person making the assessment. Perception of emotional content is a function of emotional literacy, which is discussed in a later chapter.

These available events have a clear effect on risk attitudes. Where the present uncertain situation is perceived as being similar to something else which is easy to recall, then the level of risk will be deemed to be similar to what was previously experienced. Recent and dramatic events have a disproportionately significant influence over the perception of the degree of risk associated with a new uncertain situation. It is also the case that the most memorable events (though not all) tend to be negative, leading to undue pessimism when these are perceived as indicators of the current situation.

The influence exerted by recent memories leads to a failure to take full account of the complete set of relevant experiences, and can contribute to a self-fulfilling trend. If the most recent available memory was of a risky situation whose outcome was adverse, the present uncertain situation will tend to be perceived as adverse, with a corresponding influence over risk attitude. Similarly if dramatic data is more available than usual, it will exert a biasing influence over the perception of current uncertainty, masking the proper consideration of all relevant experiences.

A good example of the availability heuristic was the reaction of the US travelling public in the aftermath of the terrorist attacks on 11 September 2001. The events in New York and Washington were so dramatic that they exerted an extremely strong influence over the attitudes of those assessing the risks of air travel, especially in the months immediately following the attacks. The normal degree of uncertainty associated with air travel still existed and was largely unchanged, but the threat level was perceived as much higher, resulting in a significant and sustained reduction in the number of people choosing to fly.

A similar effect is evident in the perception of UK parents regarding the vulnerability of children to abduction and assault. The level of concern became much higher in the 1990s following a series of high-profile cases which attracted sustained media coverage, and led parents to perceive that the risk was significantly increased. However recent research by Professor Colin Pooley of Lancaster University (reported in August 2004) based on actual data indicates that the level of abductions or assaults on children in the UK today has remained almost exactly the same since the 1940s. The only difference is the public awareness of each incident, leading to a perception of increased risk. The availability of data through the media has influenced the perceived level of threat, though the reality remains unchanged.

The availability heuristic can influence several points in the typical risk management process. For example, use of checklists for risk identification can result in memories of previous risks being activated, leading to an increased tendency to identify these same risks in the current situation. Exceptional occurrences of risks (either threats or opportunities) on the last project can result in a higher assessment of the probability of the same risk recurring on the current project, on the basis that 'it happened before so it can happen again'.

The main protection from the effect of the availability heuristic is to consciously review all available data when assessing a new uncertain situation, instead of relying on what comes easily to memory. This is the role of post-project reviews, lessons learned reports, knowledge management and so on, making previous experience available for current decision-making.

THE REPRESENTATIVENESS HEURISTIC

I am a middle-aged middle-class Englishman living in the south of England. Can you suggest what some of my characteristics might be? What automatic assumptions have you made about me?

In the same way that the availability heuristic provides a filter when an unconscious search of memory is performed, the representativeness heuristic also operates to select some data items over others as relevant reference points for assessing uncertain situations. However, where the availability heuristic gives greater weight to those items more easily accessible to the memory, a different criterion is applied by the *representativeness heuristic*. In this case a subconscious search is undertaken to match the present situation with a number of exemplars, each of which represents a group of similar situations. In common parlance, an attempt is made to pigeonhole or classify the current situation by comparing it with a small range of stereotypes (as illustrated in

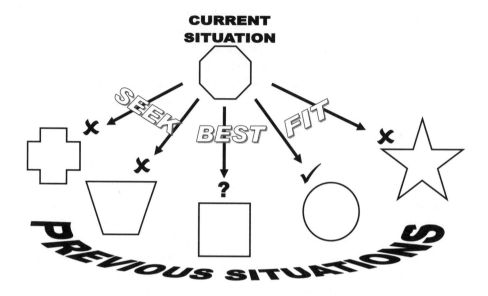

Figure 4.2   The representativeness heuristic

Figure 4.2). The closer the match between the uncertain situation and one of the stereotypical comparators, the stronger is the influence exerted by the prior experience, since it appears that what happened before is an accurate *representation* of what will happen this time. The stereotype is viewed as *representative* of the situation under consideration.

Of course sometimes stereotypes can be a useful starting and accurate point, but they could also be misleading and result in a bias of the assessment process. The direction of bias exerted by a stereotype on the perception of risk can be either positive or negative, depending on the level of risk associated with the reference situation (though this may also be influenced by the affect heuristic recently described by Slovic). If a match is made with a prior situation perceived as low-risk or offering significant opportunity, a similarly positive assessment will be more likely concerning the risk exposure associated with the new situation, leading to an optimistic risk attitude. Equally a perceived link between the current situation and a previous negative experience which involved high levels of threat will bias the risk attitude towards pessimism.

This type of heuristic is characterized by statements or beliefs which feature the words 'always' or 'usually'; for example 'All software integration projects always overrun and overspend' or 'We usually experience performance shortfalls and interface problems with equipment from this supplier' or 'This project manager always wins the client's confidence and minimizes scope changes'. When a current situation is judged to belong to the same dataset as one of these stereotypes, the starting point for the evaluation of risk is biased by the generic assessment.

The representativeness heuristic also tends to result in undue attention on those aspects of the current situation which most closely resemble the selected exemplar. At the same time, other characteristics tend to be ignored, especially where they are absent from the stereotype, producing an incomplete assessment of the degree of current risk exposure.

There are two problems with the way that the representativeness heuristic operates. The first is the natural variation which exists within populations, such that it is not 'always' true that all members of a given dataset perform in an identical manner. So even if the current situation is genuinely similar to others previously experienced, the level of risk may in fact be significantly different this time. A second problem is that items may appear superficially to be similar but may in fact not belong to the same set. The same symptoms may arise from differing underlying causes, leading to erroneous allocation of a particular instance to the wrong pigeonhole.

As a source of bias to the perception of uncertainty, the representativeness heuristic tends to result in a less rigorous assessment of risk in the current situation, arising from a reliance on the perceived similarity with a situation previously experienced. This often means that unique risks specific to the current situation are overlooked or given insufficient weight, since they did not feature in the reference situation.

The representativeness heuristic can be countered by adopting a conscious inductive examination of the situation at hand, seeking to determine its characteristics per se rather than using the subconscious and biased deductive approach of comparing with pre-existing stereotypes.

THE ANCHORING AND ADJUSTMENT HEURISTIC

Someone once told me that the population of Turkey was 38 million. What do you think? What is your best estimate of the population of Turkey?

An interesting effect has been observed when people are asked to estimate a value when they have no hard data to make a judgement. It appears that people do not make a random guess, but instead they select a starting point and then adjust their estimate from there. The subconscious thinking accompanying this process is as follows: 'The first number I think of is a good place from which to start; if any other number had been a better starting place I would have thought of that number first.' The irrationality of this thinking is evident, but it is nevertheless a powerful influence on estimating under conditions of uncertainty. This subconscious process is called the *anchoring and adjustment heuristic*, since the value first selected acts as an *anchor* for the assessment of uncertainty, around which an *adjustment* is made either up or down to reach an assessment which is regarded as realistic (see Figure 4.3).

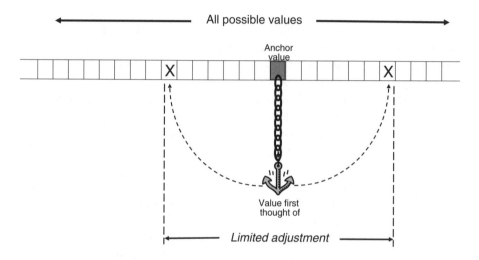

Figure 4.3   The anchoring and adjustment heuristic

As for the other heuristics, anchoring and adjustment are a means of reducing the field to be considered when addressing uncertainty. Instead of having to think about all possible values, the task is made more manageable by limiting it to the value first thought of, plus or minus some amount.

The 'value first thought of' can arise from a number of sources. For example it may be suggested by a value contained in a planning or scoping document, or a value contained in the initial formulation of the problem, or a suggestion from a colleague or comparison with prior experience. An anchor need not necessarily be a false guide to the true situation, since it can arise from an accurate source. It is, however, a dangerous method for assessing uncertainty, since the selection of the initial value is usually made subconsciously and therefore cannot be challenged.

A typical example of this heuristic in operation can be found during the generation of input data for a quantitative risk analysis model, where a typical three-point estimate requires determination of the best case (realistic minimum, or optimistic value), most-likely value and worst case (realistic maximum, or pessimistic value). Often the risk model is based on a baseline plan, which is used as a starting-point to which the effects of uncertainty are added. Of course the baseline plan contains estimates of cost, duration, resource requirement and so on, for each of the constituent elements. When an estimator is asked to produce a three-point estimate for a given element, the anchoring and adjustment heuristic results in a tendency to start with the planned value and vary around it. So duration uncertainty for a task with a planned value of 10 weeks might be reflected as a three-point estimate with a minimum of 7 weeks, a most-likely value of 9 weeks, and a maximum of 15 weeks. The initial value of 10 weeks tends to act as an anchor for the estimation of uncertainty. In reality of course the uncertainty on this task might be more significant, and the original 10-week estimate might be quite unrealistic, or could contain an excess amount of contingency. A more realistic three-point estimate for the task in this case could be 4/6/20 weeks or 10/15/35 weeks.

Another problem when the anchoring and adjustment heuristic is in operation is the tendency to underestimate the spread of possible values, with insufficient adjustment around the anchor. This can lead to a significant under-assessment of uncertainty.

Other places in the risk process where this heuristic can exert an influence include attempting to determine the required level of contingency, or setting thresholds for acceptable levels of risk exposure, or assessing the probability or impacts of specific risks. Wherever there is a requirement to select a value from a continuum and significant uncertainty exists about the 'right value', the anchoring and adjustment heuristic can influence the outcome.

The effect of the anchoring and adjustment heuristic on risk attitude is for the person making the assessment to become more reactive and less considered, with the perception of uncertainty being driven by the 'value first thought of'. If an individual makes an initial anchoring assessment that a situation is very risky and should therefore be avoided, the final risk attitude is likely to be some variety of risk-aversion, more or less. Similarly if a situation first appears to be attractive and presents significant opportunities, this anchor could lead to a risk-seeking attitude where the only variable is how much risk is actually accepted.

Overcoming the effects of this heuristic requires a conscious setting aside of any initial value or assessment which might influence the final estimate. This is easier to say than to do, as the mind can display an obstinate persistence once it has latched on to something. Telling oneself to ignore something might even reinforce the strength with which it is remembered! In this case, outside assistance may be required, for example a risk facilitator might try to remove all pre-existing cues before asking subject-matter experts to assess uncertainty or produce estimates. Alternatively outsiders might be invited to make clean estimates of values without prior knowledge of the expectations or assumptions of the original plan.

THE CONFIRMATION TRAP

'For Love is blind alday and may not see,' (*The Merchant's Tale*, Geoffrey Chaucer, 1340–1400). Research from University College London by Dr Andreas Bartels and Professor Semir Zeki in June 2004 used functional magnetic resonance imaging to measure brain activation related to maternal and romantic love, and found that activated areas included those related to a rewarding experience. But the research also showed deactivation of areas of the brain responsible for negative emotions and critical social assessment. It seems that neuroscience has proved the truth of Chaucer's assertion.

Another method for making a short-cut in the decision-making process is to assume an answer then look for evidence to support or refute the assumption. This approach is the basis of the scientific method, also known as the hypothetico-deductive method, first proposed by Karl Popper (1902–1994) along with his Falsifiability Principle. The hypothetico-deductive method begins with the postulation of a hypothesis (an educated guess that explains some phenomenon), from which can be deduced certain explicit, observable predictions. The researcher then proves or tests this hypothesis through prediction and experimentation. Observations which run contrary to those predicted are taken as evidence against the hypothesis; observations which are in agreement with those predicted are taken as corroborating the hypothesis. After gathering initial evidence the hypothesis should be modified to be able to account for all the observations, and new experiments should be developed to test the improved hypothesis. When sufficient tests have been undertaken to prove the hypothesis, it may be accorded the status of a theory (a scientifically acceptable principle which explains a vast body of facts, and is supported by an overwhelming body of evidence).

Popper's Falsifiability Principle states that it is impossible to prove something true; rather it is only possible with certainty to prove that something is false. For example, all the evidence so far may suggest that the effect of gravity makes something go vertically downwards when it is dropped, as predicted by gravitational theory. But we cannot be sure that this is always true; it would only take one instance of something going in a different direction to disprove the hypothesis.

The scientific method only works when there is genuine experimentation which is open to the possibility of falsifying the initial hypothesis. There are many examples where enthusiastic scientists have chosen to record or publish only that data which supports their preconception of 'the right answer', leading to theories which have later been demonstrated to be false as contrary evidence comes to light, and such practice is rightly condemned as unscientific.

A similar effect can occur subconsciously when people have to make decisions under conditions of uncertainty. In this more general case, the source of bias is called the *confirmation trap*. Here the person facing an uncertain situation subconsciously brings a pre-existing judgement to the task of assessing the level of risk. The preconception may be based on prior experience, or may result from one of the other heuristics mentioned above, or may be an irrational assumption. Whatever the source, the individual approaches the new uncertain situation with a feeling of some familiarity. This heuristic is sometimes also known as the *corollary syndrome*, since a prior decision has been made from which supporting evidence seems to follow.

The descriptions of other heuristics above indicate that each is a short-cut to assist in assessing uncertainty by reducing the amount of data that has to be considered. The *confirmation trap heuristic* has the same effect, but operates in a different way to reduce the dataset. When this heuristic is in operation, any contrary evidence which

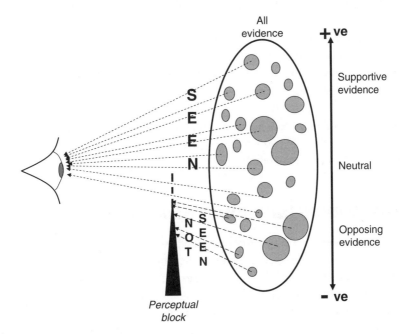

Figure 4.4   The confirmation trap

does not fit a pre-formed explanation is rejected or forced to fit, while all *confirming evidence* which is consistent with or supportive of the preferred explanation is accepted uncritically and given full weight in the decision-making process. Figure 4.4 illustrates the effect of this perceptual block in reducing the data being considered by the observer.

Examples of the confirmation trap in operation include the approach of experienced engineers to new projects. Confidence in their track record of solving technical problems on past projects can lead to an under-assessment of the degree of risk where innovation is required. The confirmation trap results in undue focus on those parts of the new project which are similar to previous experience and which are well understood, confirming the view that this new project is 'just like all the rest'. Dissimilarities are often ignored or dismissed as minor details. Similar judgements can be made by general management facing organizational change or during the due diligence process in merger and acquisition activities. Subconscious reliance on a pre-formed position results in failure to consider all the available data.

The result of the confirmation trap is to increase confidence in judgements made under conditions of uncertainty. Of course the assessment of the uncertain situation could be biased towards either pessimism or optimism, depending on the nature of the subconsciously-held prior position, but the confirmation trap leads the individual to associate greater certainty to their judgement than should be the case.

The operation of this heuristic is therefore often demonstrated by confident assessments of the level of uncertainty associated with a given situation. This is likely to lead to a more risk-seeking attitude than might normally be adopted, since the situation is perceived as less risky.

As with the other individual heuristics, the solution to the confirmation trap is to involve others in the decision-making process and to make the underlying assumptions explicit wherever possible.

UNDERSTANDING INDIVIDUAL HEURISTICS

The study of heuristics is an active area of research with wide applicability in a number of fields. Here the concern is specifically about how heuristics influence individual risk attitudes. Chapter 3 has defined risk attitude as a 'chosen response to perception of significant uncertainty', and one of the key questions is how to determine whether uncertainty is significant and in what way. This chapter has shown that heuristics operate precisely in the area of significant uncertainty, offering short-cut rules of thumb to individuals trying to assess the level of risk associated with an uncertain situation. As a result heuristics have a direct effect on individual risk attitude, influencing the chosen response based on subconscious frames of reference.

Heuristics have a number of common features. For example every heuristic is an attempt to simplify the decision-making process, to offer a short-cut by reducing the amount of data to be considered, to lead the individual more rapidly to a solution. However, the most important common characteristic of heuristics is the fact that they operate subconsciously, and are therefore not actively selected or controlled by the individual. As a result there neither can be nor should be any blame attached to biases resulting from heuristics.

The discussion above has concentrated on four of the most common subconscious sources of bias affecting individuals when they face uncertain situations, and several other individual heuristics have been identified and discussed in the literature. Treating each heuristic separately allows a focus on the specific causes of bias and improves understanding of how each particular influence operates. However, it is important to realize that heuristics do not usually act in isolation. Any individual facing a particular uncertain situation and trying to determine the appropriate risk attitude will be influenced by several heuristics at the same time. For example the representativeness heuristic may suggest a prior experience which might form a useful starting-point for understanding the new situation, then the confirmation trap could act as a filter on what evidence is considered, with the availability heuristic resulting in over-emphasis on particular data points.

While the discussion of sources of subconscious individual bias may be interesting, two further steps are required. Firstly it is important to recognize that heuristics also operate to influence groups at various levels, and this is addressed in the next chapter. But secondly, whether for individuals or groups, the important question is how these might be overcome. Of course awareness of the existence and operation of heuristics is an essential first step, but diagnosis is the not the same as cure. Part 3 details the insights offered by emotional intelligence and emotional literacy, relating to both individuals and groups, leading to Part 4 where these insights are applied to the challenge of managing risk attitudes.

CHAPTER 5

Group Risk Attitudes and Heuristics

Having addressed the influences of subconscious heuristics on risk attitudes adopted by individuals, it is now possible to consider the situation with groups. Here the proverb is true that 'The whole is greater than the sum of its parts', since the behaviour of groups is influenced by more than just their constituent individuals.

In addition to their business relationships, individuals are members of a wide range of non-work groups, including families, friendships, clubs, local communities, nations, social interest groups and so on (see Figure 1.2). Individuals in business are also organized into various groups, such as teams, committees, departments, functional communities, professional associations, divisions, companies, corporations, partnerships, alliances and so on. While each group, whether business or otherwise, has a distinct set of beliefs and behaviours which forms its culture, the scope of the discussion in this chapter is limited to groups relevant to business. A significant exception is nations, since there are indications that national characteristics may influence group attitudes towards risk, and this is also covered later in this chapter.

All groups are made up of individuals, and it is therefore inevitable that a significant factor in group risk attitudes will be some composite function of the risk attitudes of individuals in the group – but this does not entirely define how a particular group will respond or react to uncertainty. Simple examination of the behaviour of groups clearly shows that groups display distinct risk attitudes, which are chosen responses to significant uncertainty adopted by the whole group, and which can sometimes be directly contrary to the preferred risk attitudes of some or even most of the individuals making up the group.

Similarly the influences on corporate risk attitude include the combined operation of individual heuristics, but there are also covert factors which operate specifically at group level to influence the response to uncertainty adopted by the whole group. Influences on individual risk attitudes have already been discussed in Chapter 4, and this chapter considers the effect of heuristics on group risk attitude.

UNDERSTANDING GROUP RISK CULTURE

In the same way that individuals have an attitude to risk which affects their participation in the risk process, groups also have a 'risk culture' which affects the preferred approach to dealing with uncertainty. While the area of individual risk attitude has been well characterized and understood, the parallel issues relating to group risk culture are less well recognized, particularly in relation to business organizations. It is often not readily accepted that an organization can have a distinctly defined approach to uncertainty, or that it is possible for this to be determined and modified in a similar way as individual risk attitudes. This is partly driven by the wider discussion over whether an organization as an entity can have a 'company culture' or display 'organizational psychology' or 'corporate behaviour'.

The definition of culture as 'the total of the shared beliefs, values and knowledge of a group of people with a common purpose' indicates both an individual dimension and a corporate dimension. The culture of the group is determined in part by the people who make up the group, but there are also other elements which arise from the group as a whole.

Specifically in the arena of approaches to risk, it seems clear that a group can adopt a distinct risk attitude or chosen response to significant uncertainty. At the simplest level, organizations and other groups can be divided into the same categories as individuals, on a spectrum from risk-averse through risk-tolerant and risk-neutral to risk-seeking (see Figure 3.5). A range of organizational risk cultures are possible, at one extreme leading to aversion to risk, or even hostility in some cases: 'We don't have risk in our projects – we're professionals/engineers/scientists ...' This denial results in important risks being ignored, and decisions being taken without cognizance of the associated threats and opportunities. At the other end of the scale is the risk-seeking organization, and some may even become risk-addicted. A gung-ho attitude to risk will inevitably lead to disaster when the amount of risk exposure taken on exceeds the organization's ability to manage it.

There are several overt factors which drive the risk attitude of an organization, the most obvious of which is its industry sector. For example risk-aversion typically may be displayed by providers of banking and financial services, nuclear and energy sectors, and government departments. Risk-seeking organizations might include venture capital companies, the pharmaceutical and biotech sector, or marketing agencies, as well as small entrepreneurs and start-ups. The effect of these explicit drivers of risk attitude is easy to identify, and it can therefore be taken into account when monitoring the approach to uncertainty adopted by organizations in each industry sector.

Less easy to identify, however, are heuristics which affect corporate risk attitude in a hidden manner. These are underlying innate paradigms deep within the organizational psyche (that is they are 'subconscious' to the group), and often individual managers or decision-makers are unaware of their existence or influence. The most common corporate risk heuristics relate to group dynamics which operate when making decisions under conditions of uncertainty, including:

- 'groupthink' – members of a cohesive group prefer unanimity and suppress dissent;

- 'the Moses Factor' – an influential person's risk attitude is adopted against the personal preferences of group members;

- 'cultural conformity' – making decisions which match the perceived organizational ethos or cultural norms;

- 'risky shift' – the tendency of a group to be more risk-seeking than its constituent individuals;

- 'cautious shift' – the opposite of 'risky shift', when the group becomes more risk-averse than its individual members.

The following sections in this chapter address each of these group heuristics in turn, providing definitions and examples of their influence on group risk attitudes. It is important to note that these group heuristics often do not occur in isolation, and there may be a reinforcing or causal relationship between them. While this is not always the

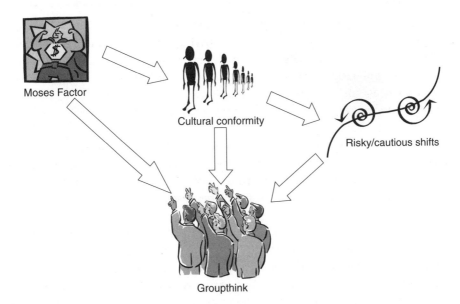

Figure 5.1   Group heuristics possible interrelationships

case, and any one heuristic can exist alone, one might imagine a situation where the influence of a charismatic leader (the Moses Factor) leads to a desire to toe the party line (cultural conformity), which in turn results in the group adopting a more extreme position than individuals might wish (risky or cautious shift), at which point the group becomes locked into the consensus (groupthink). This possible sequence is illustrated in Figure 5.1.

There is also another important factor which can influence corporate risk culture in addition to group heuristics, namely the prevailing risk culture of the society in which the organization exists. In the same way that organizations can display a coherent risk attitude, so it is possible to define a preferred approach to risk within a given national or social setting. This is also discussed towards the end of this chapter.

THE GROUPTHINK HEURISTIC

> 'So we've all agreed to approve this strategic three-year plan to expand our business into China by merging with our key competitor and introducing a new product line through the office which we'll establish next month in Shanghai. At this late stage are there any dissenters, does anyone want to voice any last-minute concerns, this is your final chance to say what you think – no? So it's agreed then, let's do it ...'

Groupthink is a mode of thinking that people engage in when they are deeply involved in a cohesive group, when the members' strivings for unanimity override their motivation to realistically appraise alternative courses of action. The term was first coined by psychologist Irving Janis (1918–1990) following the notorious 1959–61 Bay of Pigs fiasco, when members of the US Kennedy administration all agreed with the apparent consensus to invade Cuba while privately holding serious reservations.

Since its original definition, use of the term groupthink has evolved to describe a subconscious factor which blinds group members to the existence of alternative options different from the group consensus. This is different from the original Bay of Pigs situation, where participants knowingly suppressed their dissent.

Groupthink in the current understanding is therefore characterized by a subconscious desire on the part of group members to avoid confrontation, and to protect whatever consensus has been reached, not to 'speak out of turn'. While desire for consensus is a laudable aim, it can lead to suppression of dissenting opinions and failure to consider risks openly and appropriately. If it appears that the group has a settled opinion or judgement on the matter being considered, individuals with a contrary opinion will experience a covert sense of pressure to conform to the majority view, seeking safety in numbers. Expressing doubts or concerns is viewed as a sign of not belonging to the group, which is a powerful motivator especially where the group is particularly cohesive. In the same way, being part of the in-crowd provides a sense of invulnerability through shared responsibility and accountability, since the individual cannot be blamed for the decision of the whole group.

These strong influences usually operate below the level of consciousness of individuals or the group, leading to silent self-censorship which may be hidden from those who it affects the most. And since all members of a cohesive group are likely to be affected by groupthink to a greater or lesser degree, there is often no one present to offer a challenge or ask pointed questions to test the conclusions of the group.

While groupthink exerts a major influence over all aspects of decision-making, it has a particular effect on the risk attitude of a group. When facing an uncertain situation the dynamics of the group may initially lead each individual to be reluctant to express their opinion. In these circumstances it is likely to be difficult to reach a consensus on the appropriate response to uncertainty, and the group may struggle in the decision-making process. As a result, when progress appears to be made towards a settled view, the pressure against dissent increases, and the closer the group gets to a decision the greater is the tendency to maintain consensus. And whatever risk attitude is prevailing at the time that consensus is reached will tend to be the risk attitude adopted by the group and protected as 'the right approach'.

This means that groupthink tends to operate most powerfully towards the end of a decision-making process, or when some progress has been made towards establishing consensus on a preferred risk attitude in response to a given uncertain situation. There are a number of other heuristics which might come into play before groupthink and which determine what that preferred risk attitude might be. These include the so-called *Moses Factor*, cultural conformity, and risky and cautious shifts, each of which is covered in the following sections.

THE MOSES FACTOR

'If that's what Jack wants, then that's what Jack will get.' 'Who's Jack?' 'Well he is the boss, but he has lots of experience and knows what he's talking about. And he's a really nice guy, though you wouldn't like him when he's cross.'

Another key source of influence can be identified, which is related to the cultural conformity heuristic, but instead of following the prevailing style or ethos of the group or organization, this heuristic is focused around a person. Named after Moses (though other inspirational leaders could be substituted, such as Mandela, Montgomery, Kennedy or Ghandi), the *Moses Factor* heuristic operates when the group subconsciously follows the example of a charismatic person and adopts their preferred risk attitude even when it may contradict the personal preferences of individual group members. The person exerting this influence is often the group leader or a senior manager in the organization, though this is not always the case.

It is important to recognize that individuals can exercise different forms of power, each of which can result in this type of influence over the group's chosen risk attitude. Five sources of power can be distinguished, namely:

- *Referent power*. This is based on the personality of the individual, who is regarded as a role model by others. It is the strongest source of power since it derives from who the person is in themselves, rather than what they do or how they perform. Followers seek to identify with a person demonstrating referent power, choosing to follow based on trust and respect.

- *Expert power*. Based on knowledge and expertise in a relevant domain, the person exercises power and influence over others through demonstrating technical competence and specialized skill. Many senior managers in organizations have been promoted from functional roles where they excelled, and can retain this reputation even when they no longer operate in the technical domain.

- *Reward power*. Leaders often have the ability to meet the needs of others in a variety of ways, including financial, emotional, professional, status and so on. Rewards should be given which are valued by recipients, and in return for recognized performance, rather than as bribes to produce desired behaviour. People will often defer to someone in recognition of their ability to deliver such rewards.

- *Coercive power*. This is a fear-based source of power, recognizing that leaders can impose sanctions on others in the group if they fail to comply. While this may be effective in the short term it is ultimately the least effective influence since it leads to resentment and lack of motivation. Coercive power is the opposite of reward power, relying on a desire to avoid negative consequences.

- *Legitimate power*. This derives from the formal position of the leader in the group or organization, which gives rightful authority to make decisions and impose policy and direction. As a source of power, however, it may be weak since people may respect the position but not the person.

The strength of each of these sources of power will vary depending on the prevailing culture of the organization, and can also be influenced by national characteristics (see below). It is, however, important to recognize that people exert influence over others through a variety of mechanisms, and often a combination of the above factors may be in operation at the same time.

In terms of its effect on group risk attitudes, the Moses Factor may result from any one or several of the sources of power outlined above, but as with all heuristics it functions covertly. As a result, groups can be subtly influenced to adopt an approach to risk which may seem counter intuitive to its individual members. And the influence of the key person may be unintentional, rather than representing an overt attempt to manipulate the group. Indeed the Moses Factor can lead to a group's risk attitude being influenced by someone with power who is not the formal or official group leader or who does not have organizational position or status. This is particularly the case where the main active factor is referent or expert power, which is often exercised by admired or respected people with no formal position.

The Moses Factor can influence risk attitudes towards either risk-seeking or risk-aversion, depending on the perceived risk attitude of the person exercising the power. The word 'perceived' is important here, as the heuristic results in the group tending to adopt the risk attitude which they think the influential person holds – but they may be mistaken. This heuristic is best overcome through disclosure, with all key players making their preferred risk attitude explicit, followed by a stated intention to treat all views as equally valid, and a commitment to reach a true group consensus not driven unduly by the position of one person.

THE CULTURAL CONFORMITY HEURISTIC

> 'You're the new team aren't you, brought in from headquarters to improve our procurement process. I can tell, all that enthusiasm and energy – you obviously have no idea of the way we do things round here. Just slow down and go with the flow. I give it six months, then you'll be just like the rest of us.'

When a group has to deal with a novel or uncertain situation and is seeking guidance on the appropriate way to respond, reference is often made to previous experience within the group or its wider context. While this is an important part of the rational decision-making process, and it is clearly important to learn from the past, it is all too easy for the organizational context to exert an undue and hidden influence on a group facing uncertainty. In this case the group can be subject to the *cultural conformity heuristic*, which biases the group towards making decisions which match the perceived ethos or style of the organization at large, thus producing outcomes which are compliant with the accepted organizational social and cultural norms.

In this case, if the group perceives the wider organization to be unwilling or unable to accept the level of risk associated with the current situation under consideration, the risk attitude of the group will tend to be more risk-averse than it would have been without such a perception. The opposite is true, with increased risk-seeking resulting from a perception that the level of current risk exposure is below the risk threshold or risk appetite of the organization.

A powerful influence on the direction of the cultural conformity heuristic can result from the presence of a strong leader, whose views are taken by the group as defining the prevailing culture to which they should conform. If this occurs, it represents the interaction between the Moses Factor and the cultural conformity heuristics (see Figure 5.1), and the reinforcing effect of the two together can be very strong in influencing group behaviour.

Cultural conformity is described as a heuristic because it is a subconscious short-cut to assist decision-making when uncertain. Consequently cultural conformity operates covertly, affecting the adopted group risk attitude without the group being aware of its existence. Its primary danger is in reinforcing the perceived risk attitude of the wider organization, making it difficult for the organization to develop or evolve to meet new challenges. Cultural conformity ensures persistence of the legacy risk attitude, preventing the flexibility and agility which organizations need in order to respond to the constant changes in their environment. Further to this, cultural conformity maintains the *perceived* risk attitude, which may be significantly different from the *actual* risk attitude, or the risk attitude *required or desired* by the organization's leaders.

Despite its powerful influence over groups within a larger organization, cultural conformity is relatively simple to diagnose and treat, since the outcomes rarely result in significant changes or dramatic developments. In terms of the effect on group risk attitudes, the cultural conformity heuristic produces pressure for 'no change', characterized by the statement 'If it ain't broke, don't fix it', and 'We've been doing it this way for generations – why change now?' This tends to produce more conservative risk-averse attitudes in most situations, unless the prevailing corporate culture is already particularly risk-seeking.

THE RISKY SHIFT AND CAUTIOUS SHIFT HEURISTICS

> Parents of teenagers often wonder how their child can be so well behaved at home but get into trouble when out with friends. Somehow it's different when they're in a group – they do things together that they would never dream of doing on their own. It only takes one or two troublemakers for the whole group to end up doing mischief.

Evidence that a *risky shift* is occurring can be seen when a group adopts a corporate risk attitude which is more risk-seeking than would be suggested or expected from the stance of its constituent individuals. Thus even though the clear majority of group members may personally hold a risk attitude within a particular range on the spectrum (see Figure 5.2), the effect of the risky shift is for the group to adopt a risk attitude shifted towards the risk-seeking end of the spectrum (that is to the right in Figure 5.2). This can be driven by a lack of individual accountability, so that group members are less concerned about taking risks for which they will not be held personally answerable, and hence are more relaxed about allowing the group to take on a level of risk exposure which is higher than their personal risk acceptance threshold. Another common influence causing risky shift is the effect of group dynamics, where the perspective of some individuals carries more weight in the group than others. In this case if those group members who hold risk-seeking positions are more vocal and persuasive than others, or if they hold powerful positions of seniority or influence, they can draw the group towards adopting their position.

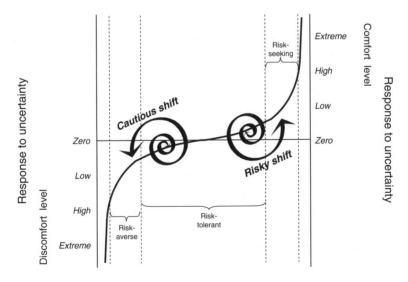

Figure 5.2   Risky shift and cautious shift heuristics

Cautious shift is the opposite of risky shift, when the overall risk attitude adopted by the group becomes more conservative than the attitudes held by its individual members. This is evidenced by a group position shifted towards the risk-averse end of the spectrum (that is, to the left in Figure 5.2). There are also a variety of drivers which can result in a cautious shift. Several of these are the converse of risky shift drivers, such as an over-emphasis in the group on personal accountability, or influential group members who are themselves risk-averse. In addition to these factors, a cautious shift can occur if no one in the group is prepared to take responsibility for risk-taking, or if the group tends to a middle course as part of the consensus-seeking process.

It should be noted that as with other heuristics, both risky shift and cautious shift are hidden influences which operate in the 'corporate subconscious'. They are not the same as a rational decision-making process during which a group moves towards a shared position based on explicit consideration of all the options. It is of course perfectly possible and proper for a group to determine that its attitude towards a given uncertain situation should be either risk-seeking or risk-averse. If this is done through an open process there is no problem. The difficulty arises when the final position taken by a group has been affected by hidden influences of which it was unaware, since the final position may be materially different from the natural outcome that would have been reached in the absence of these heuristics.

The main common feature of these two heuristics is the tendency of a group to adopt positions which are more extreme than the average position of its constituent members. They are sometimes also described as a 'vicious cycle' (risky shift) and a 'virtuous cycle' (cautious shift), though these labels betray a presupposition that a risk-seeking approach is inherently bad or dangerous ('vicious'), and risk-avoidance is always a good option ('virtuous') – which are not necessarily the case under all circumstances. However, the use of the 'cycle' image (sometimes also referred to as a circle or spiral) reflects the fact that both risky shift and cautious shift are progressive influences which develop incrementally during the functioning of a group. While the initial tendency towards a particular direction of bias may in itself be almost imperceptible, if left unaddressed the effect can gather momentum and lead inexorably towards a biased outcome. If, however, the existence of one of these heuristics can be recognized and exposed early in the functioning of the group, counter-measures can be put in place to stop further movement up or down the cycle, resulting in a group risk attitude which properly reflects the risk exposure actually being faced. This illustrates the idea that 'behaviour breeds behaviour', with the risky and cautious shifts leading to extreme behaviour unless the cycle is interrupted, which requires an active choice to adopt an appropriate risk attitude rather than the one suggested by the group dynamics.

THE INFLUENCE OF NATIONAL CULTURE

This chapter has so far addressed group dynamics factors which influence the approach to risk adopted by groups, concentrating on those hidden heuristics which bias group culture. There is, however, another significant source of influence which may have a marked effect on how a group views risk and uncertainty. This is the national context within which the group operates. All organizations exist within a particular nation, and many are multinational or transnational. Those companies with business units in several countries often comment on the different ways of working in the various locations. Similarly, differences in national culture are important issues to be addressed during mergers and acquisitions, or when companies offer products and services in other countries.

The increasingly global nature of business today means that this factor needs to be considered in a variety of contexts, including the approach adopted to risk. While a number of organizations offer cross-cultural training and support to clients, the research on national cultural characteristics towards risk is limited. This section summarizes the main research conclusions and indicates the extent to which any contribution made by national context to corporate risk culture should be considered.

Seminal research by Geert Hofstede (1928–) in the 1980s explored a number of characteristics of culture across a wide range of countries, by conducting a survey of over 116 000 IBM employees across its global organization in order to identify those factors of national culture which differentiate one nation from others. This work has continued and been updated in recent years (for example extending the surveys to include former Eastern bloc countries), with the current dataset now comprising over 140 000 people.

Hofstede summarized his research into five independent dimensions of national cultural differences, which he defines as follows:

- *Power distance* – the extent to which the less powerful members of organizations and institutions accept and expect that power is distributed unequally.

- *Individualism or collectivism* – the degree to which individuals are integrated into groups.

- *Masculinity or femininity* – the distribution of roles between the genders, either distinct or overlapping.

- *Uncertainty avoidance* – the extent to which a culture programmes its members to feel either uncomfortable or comfortable in unstructured situations.

- *Time orientation* – attitudes to time in a society in terms of gratification of needs, whether people seek instant solutions or are prepared to wait.

Hofstede also identified a range of other features of national context which can have a deep effect on the innate or preferred attitude of a national population towards uncertainty avoidance, and he categorized these under the three headings of technology, law and religion, each of which can be interpreted in terms of a greater or lesser desire to generate certainty.

Several of the five cultural dimensions can be related to the national perception of risk, but the closest element is uncertainty avoidance, indicating how far members of a culture feel threatened by uncertain or unknown events, and the degree to which people therefore seek to avoid uncertainty or ambiguity. Hofstede calculated an 'uncertainty avoidance index' (UAI) for fifty countries and three regions, and his original data is shown in Table 5.1 (together with data for 'power distance index', PDI). In his own summary of this data, Hofstede states that 'uncertainty avoidance scores are higher in Latin countries, in Japan and in German-speaking countries; lower in Anglo, Nordic and Chinese culture countries.'

Relating this to risk attitude, some have concluded that a high UAI corresponds to risk-aversion and low UAI represents risk-seeking, but more recently (2001) Hofstede has made it clear that this is an oversimplification – there is not a positive correlation. To quote directly, Hofstede states

> But uncertainty avoidance does not equal risk avoidance ... More than toward an escape from risk, uncertainty avoidance leads to an escape from ambiguity. Uncertainty-avoiding cultures shun ambiguous situations. People in such cultures look for structure in their organizations, institutions and relationships, which makes events clearly interpretable and predictable. Paradoxically, they are often prepared to engage in risky behaviour in order to reduce ambiguities ... Countries with weaker uncertainty avoidance tendencies demonstrate a lower sense of urgency... In such countries not only familiar but unfamiliar risks are accepted.

Uncertainty avoidance in Hofstede's terms represents the extent to which people prefer to avoid uncertainty through their actions and choices, or put conversely, UAI indicates the degree to which people desire certainty. People with high UAI put a high value on certainty, and this will lead them to take action to address and reduce uncertainty, in order to increase their comfort level. However, this may result in responses which are either risk-seeking or risk-averse. Some may be prepared to take inappropriate actions which increase their risk exposure as part of their search for

Table 5.1   UAI and PDI data by country/region (from Hofstede, 1982)

Country	Code	UAI score	PDI score
Greece	GRE	112	60
Portugal	POR	104	63
Guatemala	GUA	101	95
Uruguay	URU	100	61
Belgium	BEL	94	65
Salvador	SAL	94	66
Japan	JPN	92	54
Yugoslavia	YUG	88	76
Peru	PER	87	64
France	FRA	86	68
Chile	CHI	86	63
Spain	SPA	86	57
Costa Rica	COS	86	35
Panama	PAN	86	95
Argentina	ARG	86	49
Turkey	TUR	85	66
South Korea	KOR	85	60
Mexico	MEX	82	81
Israel	ISR	81	13
Colombia	COL	80	67
Venezuela	VEN	76	81
Brazil	BRA	76	69
Italy	ITA	75	50
Pakistan	PAK	70	55
Austria	AUT	70	11
Taiwan	TAI	69	58
Arab countries	ARA	68	80
Equador	EQU	67	78
Germany	GER	65	35
Thailand	THA	64	64
Iran	IRA	59	58
Finland	FIN	59	33
Switzerland	SWI	58	34
West Africa	WAF	54	77
Netherlands	NET	53	38
East Africa	EAF	52	64
Australia	AUZ	51	36
Norway	NOR	50	31
South Africa	SAF	49	49
New Zealand	NZL	49	22
Indonesia	IDO	48	78
Canada	CAN	48	39
USA	USA	46	40
Philippines	PHI	44	94
India	IND	40	77
Malaysia	MAL	36	104
Great Britain	GBR	35	35
Ireland	IRE	35	28
Hong Kong	HOK	29	68
Sweden	SWE	29	31
Denmark	DEN	23	18
Jamaica	JAM	13	45
Singapore	SIN	8	74

certainty, which is effectively a risk-seeking response. Others may over-react in their attempts to reduce uncertainty and become risk-averse. People with low uncertainty avoidance are comfortable with not knowing, and therefore are not highly motivated to address or resolve uncertainty. This can lead them to adopt a position where they recognize risk but do not feel the need to act (risk-seeking), or where they are not prepared to look for risk in case they find it (risk-averse).

In his original 1980s' publications, Hofstede identified a group of high UAI countries with a higher anxiety level, concerned about the future, driven by fear of failure, committed to hierarchical structures, resisting change and seeking consensus. This group includes what Hofstede called the 'Latin cluster', containing Italy, Venezuela, Colombia, Mexico and Argentina. On the other hand, low UAI countries appear to have a lower anxiety level, be prepared to take life a day at a time, are driven by hope of success, prepared to bypass hierarchy where justified, prepared to embrace change, and recognize the value of competition and conflict. The so-called 'Anglo cluster' match these characteristics, including Great Britain, USA, Canada, Ireland, Australia, New Zealand, South Africa and India.

Of course it would be a mistake to consider only uncertainty avoidance when seeking to understand influences on national risk culture. The other dimensions identified by Hofstede are also relevant here. For example power distance affects the degree to which people in a given national culture will feel free to identify risks, and also influences the extent of risk-taking by individuals and groups. Hofstede examined interrelationships between the various dimensions and found a positive correlation between power distance and uncertainty avoidance, as illustrated in Figure 5.3 (plotting data from Table 5.1). Taken across all 53 data points, the correlation between PDI and UAI is not strong ($R = 0.23$, that is just below the 0.05 level of significance, shown by the solid lines in Figure 5.3) suggesting that power distance and uncertainty avoidance are independent. However, when Asian, South American and African countries are excluded, PDI-UAI correlation for European and western countries is much stronger ($R = 0.78$, dotted lines in Figure 5.3), resulting from the influence of their shared cultural heritage. Other similar correlations exist and these must be considered for a full understanding of the factors influencing national risk culture.

There have been some criticisms of Hofstede's original work, which need to be taken into account when considering how much weight should be given to his conclusions. Five major criticisms are outlined below:

- The first caution arises from the *limited dataset* used by Hofstede to determine national cultural characteristics. For example, calculation of UAI was based on responses to only three diagnostic questions. These covered the following:

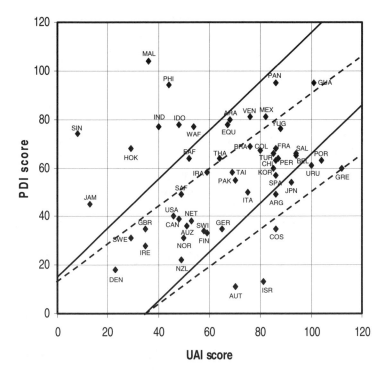

Figure 5.3 Correlating power distance index (PDI) and uncertainty avoidance index (UAI) (from Hofstede, 2001)

- rule orientation ('Company rules should not be broken even when the employee thinks it is in the company's best interests.') with answers on a 5-point scale from strongly agree to strongly disagree;

- employment stability ('How long do you think you will continue working for this company?') with possible answers of <2 years, 2–5 years, >5 years but before retirement, and until retirement;

- stress ('How often do you feel nervous or tense at work?') with a 5-point scale from always to never.

While Hofstede gives a detailed rationale on how responses to these three questions can be interpreted to give insights into the underlying approach to uncertainty, some have argued that the limited empirical database may have resulted in oversimplified inferences that may perhaps go beyond what the data can support. It is, however, creditable that Hofstede has exposed the source of his data to allow independent verification and traceability.

- A second weakness of Hofstede's work is the *age of the data*, since it was based on a survey undertaken from 1968 and 1970, and societies have changed dramatically since then (although it can be argued that the underlying cultural characteristics of a nation change more slowly as a result of that nation's 'deep history'). Some of Hofstede's conclusions are consistent with other later work, but there has been no confirmatory study which is directly comparable in scope or scale. (For example recent studies by Trompenaars on national cultural characteristics have been based on over 20 000 questionnaires, but the interpretation of this data is somewhat anecdotal without a clear underlying conceptual or theoretical framework.) Since Hofstede's conclusions are based on the original data of which some are almost 30 years old, the original interpretations may no longer be valid in the light of recent global and societal changes.

- A further limitation is the fact that Hofstede's original work was done all in *one large multinational company* (IBM) in an attempt to focus the work entirely on national cultural differences and screen out influences of differing organizational culture. This probably skewed the data but in a way which is hard to identify and correct for.

- Some equate the conclusions of the work by Hofstede and others on national culture to simplistic *stereotyping*, leading to bias, prejudice and discrimination. While stereotyping is the basis of the representativeness heuristic discussed in Chapter 4, it is nevertheless a useful short-cut to understanding basic characteristics associated with a definable group. Stereotyping can provide general data as a starting point for understanding cultural differences, and is only negative when it is focused on an individual, without recognizing that each specific individual within a cultural grouping will vary from the general or typical stereotype.

- Lastly there is the question of *multiculturalism*, which has increased dramatically in recent years as a result of globalization, and as a result monocultures are less common in either nations or organizations. This means that there is unlikely to be a single culture within a given country, although a majority perspective may dominate. Similarly many organizations are multinational, operating across a range of countries, and so they are not subject to a single cultural influence. Although local offices of multinational corporations often display distinct cultures which reflect the host country, it is less clear whether an overarching corporate culture is driven by one or more national influences, for example the culture of the country which is home to headquarters. As for many countries, most multinational corporations are not monocultures. Indeed even organizations operating wholly within a single country may have varying subcultures or micro-cultures in different departments, divisions or locations.

One of the main criticisms of work on national cultural differences is that it encourages national stereotypes to be formed. This criticism has been directly addressed by the recent research of Gilles Spony in collaboration with Hofstede. This has produced an integrative management model addressing both personality and cross-cultural differences, and which can be used for in-depth personal coaching, team development, organizational change and international working. Spony has collected data on work values (deep motivations to work) and communication styles (observed behaviours) of managers in more than 70 countries. While addressing other factors, this work has confirmed the data from the original study undertaken by Hofstede, showing that a number of aspects of national culture can be directly related to risk attitudes, and that these can be diagnosed for individuals and groups.

Spony's work particularly identifies the preferences of some individuals towards caution, an adherence to ways of working and respect for tradition when completing tasks; as opposed to the preferences of others towards independence, spontaneity and a desire to take chances. Spony's diagnostic is sophisticated, unlike the original IBM study used by Hofstede. The close correlation of results from people using the Spony diagnostic with the original data serves to directly answer some of the stated criticisms of the original work.

This indicates that the theoretical foundation of Hofstede's work holds firm and is supported by the contemporary researchers in the field of cross-cultural communication. Accordingly it is useful as a starting point to build understanding of some of the influences on national, corporate and individual risk attitudes. It is clear that an organization is likely to be influenced by the prevailing culture of the country or countries in which it operates. However, it is not possible simply to correlate corporate risk culture with national UAI score, both as a result of the limitations in the uncertainty avoidance concept, and because there is no one-to-one linkage between UAI and risk attitude. The same is true when considering possible relationships between Hofstede's other dimensions and organizational risk culture. The best that can be said is that national character probably has some influence on the risk attitude adopted by an organization and its individuals, although the extent and nature of that influence is not entirely clear.

This reinforces the key point that it is much more useful to understand risk attitudes and culture at an individual and team level than at the level of the organization or nation, although the higher levels undoubtedly have an influence.

MODIFYING GROUP RISK CULTURE

Drivers of the risk attitudes adopted by groups are many and complex, arising from external influences such as host country UAI, internal pressures such as group risk heuristics and the underlying risk attitude characteristic of the organization's industry sector – as well as the contributing effects of the risk attitudes of the individuals who make up the group. Nevertheless, in the same way that awareness of individual risk attitudes opens the door to their modification, so an organization or group which understands its preferred approach to risk and which has identified the key influences on that approach can undertake steps to modify the corporate risk culture.

As for individual risk attitudes, the existing group risk culture is not immutable. Awareness is the necessary first step towards change, and an organization can then respond to modify its corporate risk attitude to match the demands of particular situations. A strategic audit of corporate risk attitude can be undertaken to diagnose the presence and strength of various drivers of risk culture described above, defining routes to improvement and development as part of an overall change programme. This might require minor adjustments to the way the business operates, or could involve a more wide-ranging organizational redesign, aiming to make the organization alert and responsive to both upside and downside uncertainty. For example when facing a recession an organization can adopt appropriate risk-averse strategies to protect the core business while remaining alert to possible expansion or diversification opportunities that would demand the ability to take risks.

By understanding its preferred or innate risk attitude and the drivers which influence it, an organization can make the cultural changes necessary to respond appropriately to its uncertain environment in order to minimize and avoid threats while simultaneously enhancing and capturing opportunities. A powerful means of generating the required change is to develop emotional literacy across the organization, in order to encourage the ability to handle uncertainty positively. The principles and practice of emotional literacy are detailed in the following chapters (Part 3), leading to Part 4 which applies them to the understanding and management of both individual and group risk attitudes.

PART 3

Understanding Emotional Literacy

CHAPTER 6

Emotion – Definition and Relevance

Everyone experiences emotions throughout their waking and working day, and even when they sleep. Yet like the term 'risk', there is no single widely accepted definition for what we all experience. All standard dictionaries offer definitions for the term 'emotion', from 'disturbance of mind' which suggests something moderately alarming, to 'mental sensation or state' which at least begins to hint that the emotions that everyone experiences are neither positive nor negative, but are neutral. For example the fact that a particular person feels fear is only meaningful in context. If the fear is preventing the person from pursuing a course of action that would be beneficial for them, the emotion is negative. Conversely if the fear is preventing the person from doing something dangerous then the emotion is positive. Emotions in themselves have no absolute meaning, their significance is only important in relation to the objectives that people seek to achieve.

One dictionary definition defines emotions as 'instinctive feelings that arise spontaneously rather than through conscious effort, often accompanied by physiological change'. Such instinctive feelings are not reasoned or logical, but neither do individuals need to be victims of them. Whilst psychologists may differentiate between emotions, feelings, moods, temperament and other affective states, here the term 'emotion' is used to mean *all of those instinctive feelings that are held and expressed*. Further, this definition of the term emotion is used making two central assumptions:

- Emotions can be recognized, understood, appropriately expressed and managed.

- People can harness emotions to help themselves and others succeed.

EMOTION IN THE WORKPLACE

However much people may like to think that in work situations they behave logically, analysing problems and making decisions in a rational way, the reality is that emotions are always present, influencing behaviour and actions.

In just the same way that some people may feel *fear* if they need to express an opinion in front of strangers, others feel *angry* that people 'say what they think others want to hear' instead of telling the 'truth'. Emotions are at play continually, and people need to understand and deal with them in order to be truly effective.

Although many researchers have attempted to categorize emotions into a small number of basic feelings towards external stimuli, the rich English vocabulary has many words to describe how people feel. Some emotions however are so primal that they are difficult to ignore or mask. For example if someone feels *fear, anger* or *desire* in a situation it can be difficult for them to consciously over-ride the subconscious tendency to 'go with their feeling'. Less emotive words may be used for these feelings, such as *anxious, cross* or *excited*, but the effect is the same. Resultant actions that occur as a result of such emotions may be positive or negative (that is fear/anger/desire can be empowering or debilitating), but it is certain that they will affect behaviour.

Other emotions that people feel are less primal and more of a secondary response to some other situation. For example if someone feels *sad, worried, happy, joyful, guilty* or *remorseful* about a situation, there is a strong likelihood that the decisions and actions taken will reflect the emotional state of the person involved, unless they consciously manage them.

Not only do emotions drive the actions of individuals, they also affect the wider groups in which people work, and vice versa: the emotional state of colleagues affects decision-making processes if not acknowledged and managed.

Whilst the world would be a lesser place without spontaneity, the route to effective decision-making begins with individuals being cognizant of the emotions that drive them. This awareness does not make the emotion go away, although awareness and understanding can enable the choice to change, but it does provide the basis for harnessing emotions to produce results that lead towards rather than away from goals. Accordingly, it is asserted that 'If you know yourself, you won't get in the way (… of your decision-making processes)', and this is directly relevant to decision-making in general and effective risk management in particular.

THE HISTORY OF EMOTIONAL INTELLIGENCE

Although the term 'emotional intelligence' has only been part of common parlance in the last decade, the concept, as with most things, is not new.

The word emotion (like motivation) has its roots in the Latin verb 'movere', which means to move. This is consistent with the definition of emotion that links the instinctive feeling to physiological state. Psychologists in recent times have observed that there is a direct relationship between emotions and motivational states. But such a link has been recognized for centuries.

In 400 BC, the Greek philosopher Socrates (469–399 BC) argued that it is necessary to 'know thyself to be wise' and that 'the unexamined life is not worth living'. Socrates went on to state that 'Every pleasure or pain has a sort of rivet with which it fastens the soul to the body and pins it down and makes it corporeal, accepting as true whatever the body certifies.' This was perhaps the earliest published recognition that in order to understand oneself, it is necessary to understand the physiological effects caused by emotions, and also to recognize the emotional effects when we physiologically encounter similar situations in future. This link between the psychological and physiological effect of emotions is shown in Figure 6.1. A key part of emotional intelligence as described today requires people to understand the subconscious patterns they create, and if necessary to be able to interrupt or modify them.

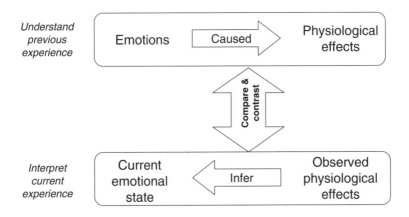

Figure 6.1   Link between the psychological and physiological effects of emotion

In 1649, the French philosopher René Descartes (1596–1650) wrote his last major book called *The Passions of the Soul* (*Les passions de l'âme*), and argued that although six basic human emotions affect all the things that people do, one can know what they are and learn how to control them. The six basic human emotions listed by Descartes were *wonder, desire, love, hatred, joy* and *sadness*, as illustrated in Figure 6.2.

Descartes claimed that 'all the others (emotions) are either composed from some of these six or they are species of them'. Like Socrates more than 2000 years before him, Descartes stressed the importance of understanding what each of these emotions [passions] feels like, as well as recognizing the physiological causes and effects in the body. If this is done, he argued that all related emotions could be understood and managed.

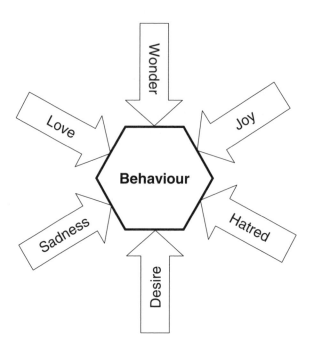

Figure 6.2   Descartes' six passions

Descartes asserted that people can become 'masters of their passions' and can 'control them with such skill that the evils which they cause are quite bearable and can even become a source of joy'. Whilst it is recognized today that not all emotions are negative, the central premise posed by Descartes is that emotions will drive people whether they want that or not, and therefore it is better to understand and harness those emotions for positive rather than negative effect.

In the last hundred years, many people have become aware of the work of the psychologist Sigmund Freud (1856–1939) in exposing the influence of the subconscious mind, and the term 'Freudian slip' is now part of everyday language. It is recognized that the subconscious has a much greater impact on behaviour than the rational thought of the conscious mind. However, the application of Freud's work in the business context has been less clear. This is in part because in the early 1900s, the study of emotions was excluded from scientific psychology because the introspective method used was deemed to be biased and subject to distortion. In addition, during the past century, people began to link success in life with a type of power where a powerful person was one with 'nerves of steel' and the capacity to be emotionally detached and cool. In such a world emotions are best kept under a tight rein. These views have changed in more recent years and it is recognized that subjective study into emotions between people is valid, and that personal power depends on having a comfortable relationship with emotions. Emotional intelligence requires that emotions be listened to and expressed in a productive way.

In 1983, the psychologist Howard Gardner (1943–) first published work to demonstrate that human beings display intelligence in a number of different ways, from the classically understood linguistic and logical-mathematical types of intelligence, through intrapersonal and interpersonal intelligences to areas such as musical intelligence. Gardner's original work described seven intelligences as shown in Table 6.1. This work was ground-breaking in raising awareness that different people learn and demonstrate their intelligence in different ways, and that the classic view of intelligence (measured by the intelligence quotient (IQ) and focused on the use of logical reasoning, rational analysis and spatial orientation to solve problems) was not the whole story. In more recent times Gardner has extended his thinking to examine the validity of inclusion of other areas including moral, naturalist and existential intelligences. This demonstrates the breadth of application of the term 'intelligence' beyond traditional interpretations, and lays the ground for inclusion of emotional aspects of the human experience as another type of intelligence.

Table 6.1   Gardner's seven intelligences

Linguistic intelligence
Sensitivity to spoken and written language, the ability to learn languages and the capacity to use language to accomplish certain goals.

Logical-mathematical intelligence
Capacity to analyse problems logically, carry out mathematical operations and investigate issues scientifically.

Musical intelligence
Skill in the performance, composition and appreciation of musical patterns.

Bodily-kinaesthetic intelligence
Potential for using one's whole body or parts of the body to solve problems or fashion products.

Spatial intelligence
Potential to recognize and manipulate the patterns of wide space as well as the patterns of more confined areas.

Interpersonal intelligence
Capacity to understand the intentions, motivations and desires of other people and consequently to work effectively with others.

Intrapersonal intelligence
Capacity to understand one's own desires, fears and capacities and to use such information effectively in regulating one's own life.

Accordingly when Peter Salovey and John Mayer in 1989 formally introduced the term 'emotional intelligence', it made real sense to people who intuitively already knew that IQ was not the only determinant of success in a business context. Many will have smiled at the caricature of the absent-minded professor who fails to succeed in everyday situations despite a high IQ. Some may also have observed, perhaps with some concern if they themselves have high IQ and a brilliant academic record, that many of the people who have succeeded in business terms, either as entrepreneurs or leaders of organizations, may not be particularly intelligent in the classical sense, but that they have *something else* that enables their success.

Some authors have concluded that traditional intelligence (as measured by IQ tests and academic qualifications in rational subjects) contributes only 20 per cent to the success a person can achieve. The accuracy of this estimate is not important. What matters is that for most people in most situations, success happens (or fails to happen) in a social context, that is involving other people.

Whilst it may be possible to research, describe and theoretically solve a problem by working alone, implementing the solution usually means bringing others along too. There are a plethora of management terms that could be used to describe this ability, from the intangible 'charisma' through to the more eclectic 'leadership'. Whichever term is preferred, all require an ability to handle one's own emotions (intrapersonally) and those of others (interpersonally); all require emotional intelligence, or a high emotional quotient (EQ) to augment IQ.

The published work of the psychologist and journalist Daniel Goleman and other authors has popularized the term 'emotional intelligence' over the past decade. There is now a wealth of literature dedicated to this theme, and designed to help individuals understand how they can become more emotionally intelligent and thus be more successful in attaining their goals.

In some respects, emotional intelligence is a 'container term' and clearly everyone has some degree of emotional intelligence that has been learned and developed more or less intuitively. The key questions are:

- How does natural, intuitive behaviour affect actions?

- How can individuals acknowledge it (at least), and continually and intentionally develop it (if they choose to)?

The chapters that follow explore the component parts of emotional intelligence as formally researched by a range of psychologists, sociologists and anthropologists, and demonstrate what this means for individuals and for groups, particularly related to decision-making in uncertain situations. Before proceeding, however, it is important to clarify the difference between emotional intelligence and another related term – emotional literacy.

FROM EMOTIONAL INTELLIGENCE TO EMOTIONAL LITERACY

The purpose of this distinction is not to argue any particular pedantic point, or to lose the importance of the subject in an argument on jargon. Either term can be used as long as individuals recognize that their ability to understand and manage their emotions is not inherently fixed, but is eminently capable of development.

The term 'intelligence' can be unhelpful when thinking of emotional development, partly because western society in recent times has conditioned people to think of IQ as being inherited, fixed or stable. However, intelligence has also recently taken on a somewhat pejorative connotation, for example in the use of the derivative 'intelligentsia'. By contrast the term 'literacy', used predominantly in an educational context, implies a skill that can be learned, nurtured and developed.

Since the early 1960s the clinical psychologist Claude Steiner (1935–) has referred to emotional literacy when working with individuals in therapy (in response to addictions) and for personal development. Steiner's work importantly relates emotional literacy to those 'ego-states' that form the core of Transactional Analysis, the technique originally developed by Eric Berne (1910–1970) in the 1950s (see Figure 6.3 and described in more detail in Chapter 7), and to the concept of giving and receiving positive 'strokes' that is the other theoretical foundation of the transactional analytic study of emotions. Steiner is a long-time teacher of emotional literacy and works with people who instinctively feel that emotional literacy training will lead to a loss of control and power in their personal and business lives. When trained in emotional literacy, these people learn that it does not merely involve an unleashing of the emotions. It also involves learning to understand, manage and control them, getting emotions to work for you instead of against you.

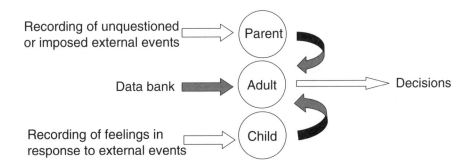

Figure 6.3   Transactional Analysis: the rational adult gets data from three sources

Others have picked up on this theme, including the psychotherapist Susie Orbach and her partners in setting up Antidote in 1995, which is a UK-based national charity to promote emotional literacy (see www.antidote.org.uk). The definition of emotional literacy used by Antidote is: 'the practice of thinking individually and collectively about how emotions shape our actions and of using emotional understanding to enrich our thinking.' This definition is important as it acknowledges the need for both individuals and groups (the collective) to be emotionally literate if the quality of thinking and decision-making is to improve.

Emotional literacy development is now widely available for individuals and teams in the workplace as well as for individuals on the psychiatrist's couch. Unfortunately to some, such development has become a consultant's growth business, and in the workplace emotional literacy (or emotional intelligence) can be seen as synonymous with qualities such as mature, stable and/or hard-working, which is to miss the point. Whilst such qualities are highly desirable in people at work, they are not the same as, nor are they necessarily indicative of the qualities of the emotional literate person which include the ability to be self-aware, empathetic and emotionally resilient. There is huge scope for development of individuals and groups in the workplace if the idea can be dispelled that being emotionally literate is mutually exclusive with power or commercial savvy.

In contrast, emotional literacy has become a significant subject matter for educational authorities and schools where children are increasingly being educated about their different feelings, how to speak about them and how to express and control them appropriately. This bodes well for future recognition of the importance of emotional literacy in business, as emotionally literate children and young people grow up and take their place in society.

For most adults, emotional development is a complex process and at a basic level involves both:

- *temperament*, which is largely inherited and is often described as *nature*, and

- *environmental factors*, which are products of experiences such as parenting, friendships, education and passive uptake of information from the media and can be described as *nurture*.

It is not necessary here to debate the relative importance of nature and nurture and relate this to emotional literacy as it is the overall effect rather than the relative impacts of the constituent parts that matter. The important thing is to acknowledge that everyone has emotions, and emotions can get in the way of decision-making and success in attaining goals. To prevent emotions having a negative effect on success, or to avoid leaving the emotional element of success to chance, the starting premise is that people are not victims of their emotions but can choose to become increasingly emotionally literate and thus take greater control of their destiny, both in their personal private lives and in the work environment.

Accordingly, and in line with the published work of educational psychologist Peter Sharp, the definition of emotional literacy used here is the ability to:

- recognize emotions,

- understand emotions,

- appropriately express emotions and

- deal with emotions

in such a way that it facilitates achievement of business and personal goals. In short, the aim is for people to know themselves well enough that they don't get in the way of the situation. This approach is powerful when adopted at an individual level, but the potential impact of emotionally literate groups is immense.

EMOTIONAL LITERACY AND RISK MANAGEMENT

It is inherent in the nature of risk management for it to be exposed to sources of explicit and implicit bias, since all elements of the risk process are performed by individuals and groups of people whose risk attitudes affect every aspect of risk management. Part 2 of this book has shown that risk attitudes exist at individual and group levels, and these can be assessed and described with some degree of accuracy. Sources of bias as a result of situational assessments (p46) and heuristics (see Chapter 4) can also be diagnosed, exposing their influence on the risk process. In this chapter we have added to the analysis of sources of bias on perception of risk by drawing attention to *emotions* that matter. Emotions can assist people in managing risk or can be a hindrance. The three influences intertwine to influence perception and shape risk attitude; this intertwining of three different influences we will refer to as the 'triple strand'.

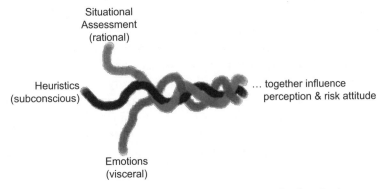

Figure 6.4   The triple strand of influences on perception and risk attitude

Where the risk attitude adopted is not conducive to effective risk management, action is required to modify attitude. Emotional literacy provides a means by which attitudinal change can be promoted and managed, for both individuals and groups.

All elements of the risk process are affected by the emotional literacy of the stakeholders, at both individual and group levels, including:

- identification of uncertainties;
- assessment of probability or likelihood of the uncertainty occurring;
- assessment of potential impact should the uncertainty occur; and/or
- deciding how to respond to assessed risks.

The assertion that emotional literacy aids effective risk management can best be demonstrated by considering a number of scenarios. Each of the four examples below presents a realistic (though fictitious) case, allowing the effect of 'the triple strand' to be considered in the context of specific elements of the risk management process, and exposing the different outcomes that might result if the people involved were emotionally literate or not. After outlining each scenario, the implications for an emotionally literate response are summarized. Readers are invited to read each scenario and think about the different ways in which situational assessment, heuristics and/or emotions might affect the outcome, before reading the summary.

SCENARIO 1

The effect of emotional literacy on identification of uncertainties

Manager A feels very *pleased* that his company's most recent project to offer services in a new geographic region has met all the business objectives set at the start. He feels *confident*, despite some opposition, that his personal leadership of the project was pivotal to the success. He asserts strongly that 'people are people' the world over and that there is no need to pay any particular attention to national cultural differences when planning such market extensions. The company is now planning to extend service provision further and is holding a risk workshop to identify the potential threats and opportunities which it will be necessary for the company to manage. Manager A is *frustrated* that some members of his management team seem to think that there is a number of threats associated with the new venture that he does not see; he wants to press on quickly and build on the success of the previous project.

Summary of the influence of perceptual factors on Scenario 1

If Manager A were emotionally literate he would recognize his feelings of pleasure in past efforts, confidence in himself and frustration that others might see potential problems that he does not see. He would also recognise that his perception was biased by his experience of success in a similar, but different, project that was recent and therefore vivid. He would be aware that this combination of situational assessment, the representatitiveness heuristic and his accompanying emotions might result in him doing the wrong thing in the risk workshop. He would recognise the need to involve others who did not have the same background and experience when identifying uncertainties and the need to look for both threats and opportunities, not just the upsides to confirm his starting position.

However, if Manager A lacks emotional literacy, he may use his position of power in the management team to close down creativity and bully colleagues into conforming with his views, not recognizing or caring about the effect he is having on others and the resultant potential effect on the latest project.

If Manager A were to misuse his power in this way, emotionally literate colleagues may recognize how this behaviour makes them feel and have the ability to control the effect of this.

SCENARIO 2

The effect of emotional literacy on accurate assessment of probability

Manager B is *resentful* of the actions of a previous colleague when they were involved in a joint business venture. This resentment was debilitating for Manager B for a long while, but a business opportunity has arisen with a new company that, if successful, would damage the business of the former colleague. Manager B is *excited about this opportunity for revenge*. Her management team has identified a number of threats and opportunities associated with the new venture. Manager B's view is that the threats are minimal (this won't happen to us) and the opportunities are massive (we can definitely make this happen).

Summary of the influence of perceptual factors on Scenario 2

Acting with emotional literacy, Manager B would understand that her past feelings of resentment and desire for revenge may result in her making the wrong decisions about the new business venture. She would realise that personal propinquity (this is of importance to her personally) was a biasing situational factor and would develop strategies to cope with their feelings when they arise. She would also recognise the supporting role that colleagues could play in countering her reactions.

An emotionally illeterate Manager B may be able to convince her colleagues that she is right about the assessment of probability of the risk identified, unaware that her assessment is driven by the personal nature of her past experience and her emotion-charged memories associated with this experience.

Emotionally literate colleagues may be able to recognize the feelings of Manager B and find ways of helping her see that it is not sensible to jeopardize the new venture by biasing decisions based on feelings.

SCENARIO 3

The effect of emotional literacy on accurate assessment of impact on objectives

Manager C is the sole shareholder in a company that made a loss in the last financial year due to an investment made in a new product that, to date, has not met sales targets. The causes of the disappointing results were due to changes in market conditions that could not have been foreseen or managed by the company. A new opportunity has been identified to design a further new product to meet a market need. Investment appraisal has shown that the initiative should pay back the initial investment of £2M within 12 months of product launch with an ongoing contribution to company profits of £5M/annum from this product line. Manager C is keen that on this occasion the team identifies all the potential threats and assesses their probability of occurrence and impact should they occur, as he is *frightened* that the company is going to make another expensive mistake that may 'take the company down'. The team has identified a long list of potential threats, assessed the probability of each and is assessing the impact should each occur.

Summary of the influence of perceptual factors on Scenario 3

If he is emotionally literate, Manager C would recognise and acknowledge that his fear of failure may result in him overplaying the impact of threats on objectives for the new venture. A recent situation with a disappointing outcome tends to bias assessment of probability (more likely) and overplay the impact (would be even worse than last time) so he would recognise the value of colleagues in balancing this view and providing more objective evidence with which to evaluate the new opportunity.

Lack of emotional literacy may mean that Manager C might try to convince colleagues that the project is so risky that it should not be pursued, thus pandering to his fear and preventing the company from taking the opportunity.

Emotionally literate colleagues may be able to counter the fears of their boss, or at least be able to acknowledge his position and deal with their own feelings in a rational way.

SCENARIO 4

The effect of emotional literacy on risk response decisions

Manager D has just joined a new company as Health and Safety Manager. At her previous company, an employee suffered a fatal injury and the resulting enquiry criticized the management for failing to provide adequate supervision for the activity being undertaken. The employee that died was a personal friend of Manager D and she still *grieves* the loss and *blames herself* for the situation although it has been explained many times that she was not actually personally responsible in any way. The new company is building a new facility and Manager D is leading the hazard and operability (HAZOP) studies for the development.

Summary of the influence of perceptual factors on Scenario 4

An emotionally literate Manager D would recognise that her grief and guilt may bias her assessment of the hazards in the new situation. She would understand that the strong memory of the major impact in her previous company was biasing her judgement about the likelihood of a similar situation happening and she would seek the advice of other colleagues to support her and bring objectivity to the assessment.

Without emotional literacy Manager D may have enough influence to impose her views on the other HAZOP team members, and result in inappropriate safeguards being made.

Emotionally literate colleagues may be able to support Manager D to the extent that her grief does not interfere with her ability to make judgements in future.

CONCLUSION

The importance of being able to recognize, understand, express and manage emotions as a means of controlling behaviour has been recognized for centuries as expressed by philosophers, psychologists and educators alike. In recent times, writers have popularized the fact that success in both a personal and business context requires emotional as well as traditional intelligence. A significant body of evidence also exists to demonstrate that emotional intelligence can be developed where there is a desire to do so, and that accordingly people can become emotionally literate.

Decision-making is an activity that consumes a large percentage of time for many individuals and groups, particularly in the workplace, and this is definitely the case for people involved in the discipline and profession of risk management. However, decision-making in uncertain situations is affected by the numerous sources of explicit and implicit bias as described in Part 2, and these biases exert a significant influence over individual and group risk attitudes. This chapter has asserted that another significant contributor to risk attitude is the emotional state of the individual or group involved, and therefore development of emotional literacy will have a direct effect on the efficacy of the risk management process.

The remainder of Part 3 focuses on a more in-depth examination of the component parts of emotional literacy for individuals in Chapter 7, followed by examination of the application of emotional literacy to groups in Chapter 8.

CHAPTER 7

Emotional Literacy for Individuals

'Something we were withholding made us weak, until we found out that it was ourselves.' This quotation from the poem 'The Gift Outright', written by American poet Robert Frost (1874–1963) in 1942 and recited at the 1961 inauguration of US President John F. Kennedy, is directly relevant to the development of emotional literacy. Emotionally literate individuals are able to recognize, understand, appropriately express and deal with the emotions that they experience both psychologically and physiologically. In doing so they are able to use their instinctive feelings to help both themselves and others succeed in the tasks they set themselves. Armed with this ability people no longer need to weaken themselves by letting their emotions manage them, rather than taking control.

TRANSACTIONAL ANALYSIS AND EMOTIONAL LITERACY

In Chapter 6, the link was made between emotional literacy and the pioneering work of Eric Berne on Transactional Analysis. At the heart of Transactional Analysis is the concept that within each person there exist three 'ego-states' or 'life-states': the Parent, the Adult and the Child. Every interaction that an individual experiences is played out from one of these ego-states. Critically, this is the case whether the interaction really happens with another person, or whether it is played out in the mind as internal self-talk; the brain records a memory whether interactions are real or imagined. Only the Adult state is rational, taking information from all possible sources and making a considered response (see Figure 6.3). Responses that are most effective when making decisions in uncertain situations undoubtedly come from the Adult, but in many cases this does not happen and an individual reacts from the Parent or Child state.

Interactions from the Parent state are based on unquestioned or imposed external *events* that were experienced in early life, things that were said or demonstrated by anyone in influential parental-type roles. Transactional Analysis has differentiated between the data held by the Parent state as Critical Parent and Nurturing Parent. These labels clearly describe the sort of memories or 'tapes' that one has recorded in response to early management, from 'Go and clean yourself up, cleanliness is next to Godliness' or 'Clear your plate, there are millions of starving people in the world', to

'Please don't do that, I'm worried you'll hurt yourself.' Whilst fortunately for most people the tapes that were recorded were done for good reasons in the first instance, it does not stop slavish adherence to them being inappropriate in the future.

In contrast to the Parent state, interactions from the Child state are based on the *feelings* experienced in response to external events. These tapes are made simultaneously with those in the Parent state and mean that whenever a similar situation happens at any time in the future, immediately the same feelings are invoked. As most Parent state tapes are dealing with what to do or what not to do, how to do something or how not to do something, the Child state tapes are the small person's emotional reaction to that experience.

All this becomes very relevant on examination of four possible 'life positions' that are borne out of these early sources of data. Life positions are automatic responses. They are conclusions that the brain draws from past experiences unless over-written by a different picture.

Firstly, most very young children adopt the life position '*I'm not OK, you're OK*' as their parental figures correct, cajole and reinforce what they are doing wrong, but do it with care and accompanied often by 'positive physical strokes'. According to Berne's research, a significant majority of children do not move from this position. Instead they carry it forward into adult life becoming the sort of person whose initial reaction to every situation is that they are at the mercy of others and that they need constant recognition and support to feel that they are OK.

Others move from this first to the second life position of '*I'm not OK, you're not OK*'. This position tends to be adopted where the critical and nurturing parenting continues but where the physical positive strokes gradually reduce and perhaps stop, for example in the case where the family situation is not tactile. Although the growing child may be happy at a conscious level, what is recorded at a subconscious level is that life is an ordeal to be survived alone. Again, some children carry this position through to adult life becoming the sort of person who sees fault in everyone, even themselves. Life becomes a continuation of the ordeal and physical and mental struggle they perceived in childhood.

Some move from the first or second to the third life position of '*I'm OK, you're not OK*'. This position is evidence that the young person has learned how to give themselves positive reinforcement so that although 'Life is tough' then 'I'm tough too'. The small percentage of people who are reported to carry this life position through into adulthood are likely to collect people around them who will reinforce their position as in the case of 'yes men'.

University of Chester, Queen's Park Library

Title: Performance strategy : complete text, paper P3 / CIMA.
ID: 36148222
Due: 26-03-18

Title: The essentials of risk management /
Michel Crouhy, Dan Galai, Robert Mark.
ID: 36092189
Due: 26-03-18

Title: Understanding and managing risk
attitude / David Hillson and Ruth Murray-
Webster.
ID: 36056959
Due: 26-03-18

Total items: 3
05/03/2018 12:19

Renew online at:
http://libcat.chester.ac.uk/patroninfo

Thank you for using Self Check

248

It is easy to see that all of the first three life positions as described could significantly hinder the development of emotional literacy as the rational judgements and decisions made by the Adult state are overpowered by the irrational subconscious influences of the Parent and Child.

Berne's work showed how individuals can choose to make the step change from one of the three life positions that represent unchallenged early life experiences based solely on feelings, to a position based on thought and faith that is '*I'm OK, you're OK*' (see Figure 7.1). The move to the fourth position requires a person to build and maintain self-esteem by proving their worth to themselves, whilst simultaneously dispelling the thoughts that trigger emotional responses that other people are 'not OK'. A no-blame culture is required: no blame of self or others.

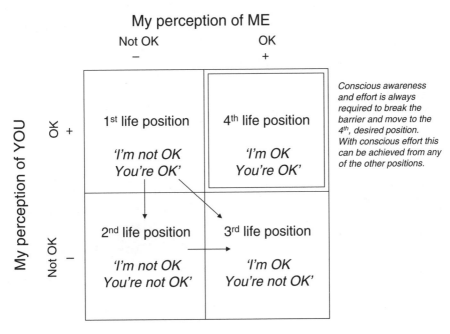

Figure 7.1   Interplay of Transactional Analysis life positions

Some children are helped in early life to find that they are OK by repeated exposure to situations in which they can prove their worth to themselves and others and hence move from the first to the fourth life position with ease. Others are not so fortunate and the transformation to hold a fundamental perception of the world that there is good in everyone takes conscious effort over time. Many people need support from friends, a coach or a therapist to make this move.

However, this fourth life position '*I'm OK, you're OK*' is a necessary and fundamental starting point for emotional literacy.

OPEN LOOP SYSTEM

The human brain is quite obviously a complex organ. It is widely understood that the part of the brain that differentiates humans and some other higher-order mammals from other species is the neo-cortex. Representing approximately two-thirds of the brain mass of a typical human, the neo-cortex is the rational, logical centre of the brain, the part that makes humans superior in terms of abstract and creative thought. Divided into two parts, commonly referred to as left and right brain, the neo-cortex has become the part of the human brain that most people would relate to the skills and behaviours necessary for business management in general, and for the management of risk specifically.

However, the neo-cortex is not the whole story. The pioneering work of neuroscientist Dr Paul MacLean in 1966 has shown that the human brain is actually made up of three distinct evolutionary parts, built over time. The three parts, which MacLean calls the Triune Brain, are really three interconnected biological computers.

The structure of the Triune Brain is shown in Figure 7.2, and can be envisaged using this simple three-part physical illustration:

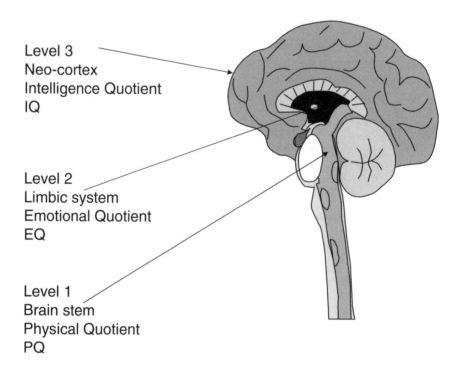

Level 3
Neo-cortex
Intelligence Quotient
IQ

Level 2
Limbic system
Emotional Quotient
EQ

Level 1
Brain stem
Physical Quotient
PQ

Figure 7.2   A depiction of the Triune Brain (adapted from Paul MacLean)

1.   Hold your left arm up with the hand at eye level and with the fingers extended

This represents the most basic part of the brain, the brain stem and cerebellum that controls all automatic bodily functions such as breathing. Labelled the archipallium or reptilian brain by MacLean, the brain stem produces rigid, obsessive, compulsive, ritualistic, paranoid behaviour. It is essential for those things that require automatic function, like the heart to beat. It also governs the 'fight, flight or freeze' reactions that everyone has in response to a perception of fear and danger.

As described in Chapter 3, a risk attitude can be defined as a 'chosen response to uncertainty that matters, driven by perception'. In some circumstances the perception of uncertainty will lead people to react entirely from the reptilian brain with a fight, or flight or freeze reaction. This is normal behaviour, but not necessarily effective behaviour. Awareness is the first step to development of more appropriate responses.

2.   With your left arm still held up, make a fist with your left hand

This represents the emotional centre of the brain or the limbic system. Labelled palleomammalian by MacLean, the limbic system is the primary seat of emotion and of emotion-charged (affective) memories. Basically, the limbic system only sees the world as either agreeable or disagreeable and it seeks to avoid pain and/or repeat pleasure. This part of the brain creates dilemmas for the rational human being, and results in the need for emotional literacy.

3.   With your left arm still held up with the hand in a fist, grip the left fist with your right hand

This represents the position of the neo-cortex as the third evolutionary stratum, the most developed part of the brain labelled the neopallium by MacLean. Without the neo-cortex a human would be a vegetable, incapable of any functions other than those to sustain actual life. However, it is the limbic system, a lower order brain that is the 'seat of all value judgements' made by a person. It is the limbic system, not the neo-cortex, that decides whether an idea is good or not; hence the need for an individual to gain understanding and control of the emotional as well as the rational part of their brain.

In *Primal Leadership: Learning to Lead with Emotional Intelligence* (Daniel Goleman, Richard Boyatzis and Annie McKee) the concept of the limbic system, or the emotional centre of the human brain as an 'open loop', is discussed. This concept is of foundational importance to the development of emotional literacy as it demonstrates that in contrast to 'closed loop' systems such as the human circulatory system that regulates itself, 'open loop' systems are affected by and regulated by largely external influences. This means that for emotional stability, most people rely on connections with other people.

This reliance on others for stability makes the fourth Transactional Analysis life position of '*I'm OK, you're OK*' more difficult to achieve yet even more important. The feedback received by the brain, whether it is intentional or not, is registered as real. It is critical that feedback reinforces 'I'm OK, you're OK'. How a person treats themselves, treats other people and is treated by others all have an impact on behaviour.

A MIND-SET OF CHOICE

Another prerequisite for emotional literacy is a mind-set that truly believes that individuals can choose their attitude to situations, that no single response is mandatory if we are prepared to accept the consequences of our choices. Chapter 1 defined the term 'attitude', making it clear that in all things attitudinal (including risk attitudes) the position an individual adopts is based on either conscious or subconscious choice and that even those people who believe that their responses are inherently fixed are in fact choosing to reinforce a previous position, thus choosing not to change.

Emotional literacy first requires recognition of feelings and emotions so that understanding can be achieved. From this position of understanding people can choose what to do next. In practical terms the choice of how to respond to a given situation is not obvious if there is no recognition and understanding of the causes of the underlying emotional state.

Linking this back to the Parent, Adult and Child ego-states within each person, individuals have the ability to either *react* from the Parent or Child ego-state without any understanding of why the reaction happened or how it could be changed, or to *respond* from the considered position of the Adult ego-state which rationally takes into account the Parent and Child tapes and allows a choice to be made (as illustrated in Figure 6.3).

The central thesis of this book is that the attitudes that people choose and hold in response to uncertain situations can be understood and managed. The decisions that people make and the behaviours that they display may appear rational and logical, but they are in fact driven by a part of the brain that is only concerned with avoiding pain or repeating pleasure. The concepts of the Triune Brain and the open loop nature of the limbic system help to explain why it is important for people to be able to understand their emotional reactions and responses as a basis for making more logical and rational choices. Transactional Analysis and the fourth life position of '*I'm OK, you're OK*' provides one way for individuals to begin to analyse their own behaviour and expose the internal driving forces behind the outward expression.

COMPONENT PARTS OF INDIVIDUAL EMOTIONAL LITERACY

Although there is no absolute agreement between authors on the features that together make an emotionally literate person, there is considerable overlap and enough synergy to draw conclusions about the critical dimensions. The dimensions of emotional literacy related to some of the main diagnostic tools are outlined in the Appendix, but in this section the generally agreed component parts are identified and mapped to the four major elements of emotional literacy, namely:

1. recognize emotions

2. understand emotions

3. appropriately express emotions

4. handle emotions.

These component parts are listed in Table 7.1, and each component is then detailed in the sections below, together with how they relate to risk management. This table does not represent a single diagnostic tool for assessing emotional literacy, but nevertheless is a meaningful composite of the components contained in the various available diagnostic frameworks.

Table 7.1   Component diagnostic elements of emotional literacy for individuals

1. Recognize emotions
- Self-awareness
- Empathy
- Organizational awareness
- Trust

2. Understand emotions
- Relative regard
- Personal power and self-confidence
- Flexibility/behavioural adaptability

3. Appropriately express emotions
- Goal directedness and emotional self control
- Personal openess and emotional honesty
- Assertiveness and conflict handling
- Optimism
- Constructive discontent

4. Handle emotions
- Intentionality/impulse control
- Emotional resilience/stress tolerance
- Interdependence
- General health and quality of life

1.   RECOGNIZE EMOTIONS

The first step to emotional literacy is an ability to recognize the existence of emotions in self and others. This has four essential components: self-awareness, empathy, organizational awareness and trust, as described below.

Self-awareness

Central to emotional literacy is the ability to be self-aware, to recognize one's own feelings accurately. All the diagnostic tools for emotional intelligence and emotional literacy include a self-assessment element. Often this self-assessment is balanced with feedback from others, but in the final analysis, an individual must be able to accurately recognize their own emotions in order to be able to move forward along the path to emotional literacy.

One of the main emotional literacy tools notes that accurate self-assessment is highly correlated with effective performance. Self-assessment is where people must start.

Empathy

Being aware of self is only half of the story. Being aware of others and being able to intuit what they are feeling is also essential. This social awareness, often called empathy, requires listening with all the senses and is really the building block for all that follows. In making judgements about self and others, it is critical to remember that reality is not an absolute but is merely a representation of what a person perceives at the time. One of the key tenets of the American/Polish semanticist Alfred Korzybski (1879–1950) is that 'the map is not the territory'.

Organizational awareness

Another aspect of recognizing emotions is the ability for organizational awareness as a basis for understanding the wider cultural and political aspects that affect the behaviour of groups. This aspect of emotional literacy for groups is discussed further in Chapter 8 and builds on Chapter 5 where the effect of group processes and behaviour on risk attitudes was examined.

Awareness and risk management

There is now a growing recognition within those groups that study risk and behaviour in risky situations that the combination of motivational and emotional factors influencing risk attitudes tend to be specific to individuals rather than being true for all people everywhere. As a result, it is important for each individual to be aware of their own set of influences.

Writing in 1987, Lola Lopes comments that

> Psychologists who study risky choice don't talk about a surprisingly
> large number of factors that are psychologically relevant in choosing
> among risks. Words such as fear, hope, safety, danger, fun, plan,
> conflict, time, duty and custom are not to be found in the theoretical
> vocabulary, nor can these words be given meaning in psychophysical
> or rational theories (including Expected Utility Theories and Prospect
> Theory).

Paul Slovic et al (2004) confirm that 'There are two fundamental ways in which human
beings comprehend risk: the analytic system using formal logic and normative rules,
and the experiential system which is intuitive and not always accessible to conscious
awareness.' Slovic's experiential system is defined by the 'affect heuristic', which is a
subconscious process that evaluates risks and decisions based on the underlying
feeling of goodness or badness as perceived by the individual. As a major player in
decision research and the rational, scientific approach to risk, it is significant that
Slovic goes on to comment that 'Proponents of formal risk analysis tend to view
affective responses to risk as irrational. Current wisdom disputes this view.'

Other authors have commented that it is human behaviour rather than processes
or procedures that are the risky factor in decision-making. As far back as the 1978 BBC
Dimbleby Lecture on 'Risk', Lord Rothschild advocated that it was necessary 'to go
inside the head of the beholder and understand how he or she sees the situation that is

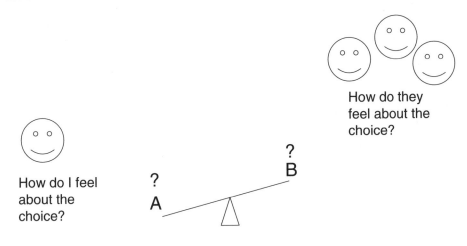

How do they
feel about the
choice?

How do I feel
about the
choice?

What will we choose and why?

Figure 7.3   The need for awareness of self and others

thought to be risky. What is done about the risk depends entirely on how the person sees it.'

Given this information, and as illustrated in Figure 7.3, it is clear that being able to recognize those instinctive feelings that drive behaviour in oneself and in other people is a necessary first step in understanding risk attitudes and managing risky situations.

Trust

To complete the challenge of recognizing emotions, the feature of emotional literacy that is generally labelled trust is necessary as a means of allowing the brain to have confidence in the data it perceives about self and others. The term 'trust', like many of the other features of emotional literacy, has more than one aspect. It relates to:

- *Self-trust* – that behaviour will be consistent, coherent and in line with inner values.

- *Trustworthiness of others* – that another individual can be relied upon to act with integrity and transparency.

- *Propensity to trust* – the degree to which a person tends to trust others around them, particularly where concrete evidence of trustworthiness is not available. This dimension is labelled 'trust radius' by some authors.

Without trust expressed in these three ways, accurate assessment of emotion and prediction of emotion-driven behaviour is difficult. However, everyone has experienced the disingenuous person or the person so motivated by 'saying the right thing' that it is then impossible to find the true path forward. In this situation it would be easy for a trustworthy and trusting person to be naïve and gullible. The emotionally literate person at least recognizes their own feelings and emotions in such a situation and maintains a healthy balance between trusting too much and too little; that is, is disposed to trust but is also careful to take care of oneself in relation to others. This requires the following questions to be answered:

- Do I trust me?

- Can I trust you?

- Will I trust you?

- How will I feel and respond if my judgement about you is proved to be wrong?

2.   UNDERSTAND EMOTIONS

If the first step along the road to emotional literacy is an ability to recognize and define emotions in self and others, the second step is to understand those emotions as a basis for being able to express and manage them appropriately. The key elements here are relative regard, personal power and self-confidence, and flexibility.

Relative regard

It is possible to recognize an emotion, for example that a person is feeling angry about a situation, and perhaps even to understand theoretically why they are feeling angry, but yet fail to really understand the situation from their point of view. In other words one can easily fail to empathize. When individuals cannot see situations through the eyes of another they risk adopting a '*You're not OK*' attitude. Similarly for self, it may be possible to recognize a feeling of guilt, but not really understand and acknowledge the cause of the feeling. As a result the feeling is pushed away as something negative, rather than being acknowledged as real and something to be dealt with. In this situation an '*I'm not OK*' position is adopted. The '*I'm OK, you're OK*' position is found when both self-regard and regard for others is displayed. This relative regard is not the same thing as 'liking what you see and what people do'. Many parents may remember saying to a loved one 'I love you, but right now I don't like your behaviour.' Separating

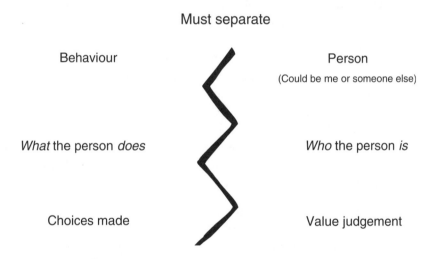

Must separate

Behaviour	Person
	(Could be me or someone else)
What the person *does*	*Who* the person *is*
Choices made	Value judgement

To achieve accurate assessment of situations

Figure 7.4   The importance of regard for self and others

behaviour from the person helps to understand the behaviour. Moreover, understanding behaviour requires separation of what a person does from who a person is, as shown in Figure 7.4. Regard for self and regard for others that is unconditional on behaviour is necessary for emotional literacy to be developed.

Relative regard and risk management

Relative regard is directly relevant to risk attitudes. Value is often associated with the adoption of particular risk attitudes in particular situations. This may be as simple as an individual thinking they are right and others are wrong to be risk-averse with a financial investment, or may be associated with thinking that risk-seeking behaviour is of greater value in an entrepreneurial business context. The task of understanding risk attitudes and managing them will always be easier if the risk attitude, or what the person has chosen to do in a particular uncertain situation, is separated from any judgement about what that choice may mean about who the person is. Regard for self and others is a necessary platform for accurate assessment of attitudes and situations, and accordingly it is pivotal to emotional literacy.

Another specific area where relative regard has a direct impact on risk management is during a creative process such as brainstorming. When using a technique such as this for risk identification, the quality of the output (all knowable risks identified) is directly related to the quality of the input. The process is compromised if individuals limit themselves through low self-regard or limit others by using overt or covert put-downs. It is clear that incomplete risk identification is not good for risk management and that human aspects have a direct part to play in this process.

Emotionally literate participants in a risk management process will understand where their emotions and the emotions of others may be the cause of an uncertainty, or represent a risk itself. Examples could be:

- *Emotion as a cause of a threat* – for example a person who is a key resource for a project is anxious about a personal situation. This may cause them to be absent from work at a critical time which in turn would cause a delay to the project end-date and major problems with stakeholder satisfaction.

- *Emotion as a cause of an opportunity* – for example two members of a team begin a romantic, personal relationship. This may cause them to want to be at work together for longer periods of time than usual which would enable some critical activities to be completed ahead of plan.

- *Emotion as a threat* – for example an employee contravenes safety regulations and the regulator takes action to restrict operations which has caused a delay to a delivery to a key customer. The customer may be very angry resulting in them transferring their allegiance to a competitor.

- *Emotion as an opportunity* – for example a husband and wife couple have decided to move their home and children to a foreign country. The children may be very excited and motivated to learn the new language and make new friends and make the move positive for all the family.

Emotion can also be a direct or indirect effect of risk, that is the thing that matters if the uncertainty occurs. A direct example would be in a situation where a calm disposition and cool head was required for a negotiation with a foreign government. Any uncertainty that would affect the ability for the negotiator to remain calm would be a risk with a direct emotional effect. Indirectly, there are many situations when the effect of one risk occurring would cause a person to become emotionally upset in some way which would directly effect objectives – such instances of emotion-related secondary risks are commonplace, but are rarely explicitly defined by the risk management process.

Emotionally literate individuals will also recognize and understand where feelings will be influential either in supporting a risk response, such as pity for a person that results in greater support, or as a hindrance to such a plan of action, such as anger at past actions causing a person to withhold cooperation.

The links between risk management and emotion are many. Relative regard for self and others is a foundational requirement for management of these links.

Personal power and self-confidence

Directly related to self-regard, the degree to which an individual accepts and values themselves is the dimension of emotional intelligence which can be described as 'personal power'. Alternatively described as self-confidence or self-esteem, people who display high levels of personal power believe they are in charge of their own destiny, rather than seeing themselves as passive or powerless victims of circumstances; they believe they can make a difference, and therefore they do.

Personal power should not disregard others. It should be an '*I'm OK, you're OK*' position which does not fear other people, but neither does it seek to overpower or ignore them. Having personal power is not the same as having legitimate, reward or expert power (as discussed in Chapter 5). Many people can exert power and influence over other people and situations because of their job title, expert knowledge or history in a situation. People with high levels of personal power have the self-confidence to know whether and where they can make a difference. They also have the self-confidence to do so and the humility to understand that others are bringing their own contribution to the proceedings. The concept is highly correlated with the referent power that is an essential element of being an effective project manager.

Personal power and risk management

There is an interesting connection between the process of developing personal power and risk attitudes. One of the ways of developing personal power is to set challenging targets and then achieve them. The process of achievement builds confidence to try the next stretch target: it is a virtuous cycle. Work by personality-focused psychologists who adopt a personologist view of the psychology of risk has shown that choices that individuals make are linked not only to the person's assessment of the probability of success or failure, but also to the satisfaction they perceive they will gain from achieving the challenge. Some people would rather fail at a challenging task (risk-seeking) than succeed at an easy one (risk-averse). People with high personal power will tend to be achievement-motivated and therefore will tend to perceive their probability of success more favourably than people with a lower achievement motivation and lower levels of personal power. In situations where the uncertainty is caused by lack of knowledge (epistemic ambiguity) rather than because the situation is inherently uncertain, like throwing a dice (aleatoric variability), this perception of probability of success is a significant factor in actual success. People who believe they can succeed in opening up their brain to produce drive and creativity do so. Success can breed success in the right environment. Some would say that 'people make their own luck'.

Formal studies examining risk-taking and achievement motivation have used games of pure chance and have shown that achievement-motivated people prefer the shortest odds they can get – the safest bet rather than the large prize with a low probability. This is because they do not seek risk where they do not feel they can make a difference through their own efforts. In further studies published by Bown et al in 2003, the 'lure of choice' heuristic was described, suggesting that 'people often prefer to obtain an outcome by making a choice, rather than allow it to be predetermined or decided by chance, even where making a choice does not improve the outcome'. In individuals with high levels of personal power, this 'choosing to choose' phenomenon is seen where the choices are limited, as the process of choosing brings a perception of control over the situation. Where there is too much choice, such individuals will probably not bother to choose unless they believe the choice can be influenced by them personally. People with low personal power are unlikely to have the confidence to choose and may prefer pre-determined outcomes or choices made by others to which they will commit, but for which they will not be personally accountable.

In situations where an uncertain situation is typified by ambiguity and not 'pure chance', it is reasonable to assume that high levels of personal power and self-confidence or esteem will fuel risk-taking and push the prevailing risk attitude towards the risk-seeking end of the spectrum (see Figure 3.5).

In terms of understanding emotions, it is important that people can understand their personal drive and motivation in a risky situation and be able to describe (to themselves at least) how they feel now about the situation, and how they will feel afterwards given either a positive outcome or a negative outcome. This understanding will help their decision-making and help them focus on the drivers of others in the group.

Flexibility or behavioural adaptability

So far the influences of self-regard, regard for others and personal power/self-confidence have been related to understanding emotions and to the effect on decision-making in risky situations. These dimensions build on the self-awareness, awareness of others, empathy and trust elements needed to recognize emotions. The final element of emotional literacy that needs to be explored before moving on to the dimensions related to appropriately expressing emotions is the one of flexibility, or behavioural adaptability.

The importance of the '*I'm OK, you're OK*' life position in the earlier dimensions has been shown and this is no less the case with flexibility. People who adopt an 'I'm not OK' position tend to be inflexible or rigid, clinging to what they know and believe and to their habitual patterns from fear because they do not value themselves. People who adopt a 'You're not OK' position display a similar inflexibility but this time because they are fearful of others and what might be done to them.

An emotionally literate person will recognize and understand where their tendency is to act in an habitual and rigid way, and will also understand underlying reasons. They will recognize the physiological effects triggered by the prospect of behaving differently from usual, and be able to understand why this is the case. This understanding then gives them the raw material to be able to explore ways to become more comfortable with change.

Flexibility and risk management

The effect of inflexibility on decision-making in risky situations is obvious: such a trait will almost certainly trigger risk-aversion. In some situations this will be appropriate. Habitual behaviour is not always counter-productive and in many situations it provides the baseline from which people can be creative and effective. For example it is difficult to do creative writing straight into word-processing software if the process of typing is not habitual. Similarly, a person who has not habitualized the process of calculating odds and optimal stakes on a horse-race is unlikely to engage in the gamble, whereas a person who has attained that skill as a free-flowing part of them is more likely to take the risk. It is well known that particularly creative skills such as musical improvisation are only possible when the basic technical skills of the craft are deeply habitualized. The same principles hold true for creativity in the business environment.

In some situations it will be appropriate for a person to interrupt and modify habits that are counter-productive. In other situations, the habit can be left uninterrupted. The ability that separates the emotionally literate person from the rest is the recognition of where the habitual behaviour is sub-optimal in relation to the goal and being able to do something about it, as depicted in Figure 7.5.

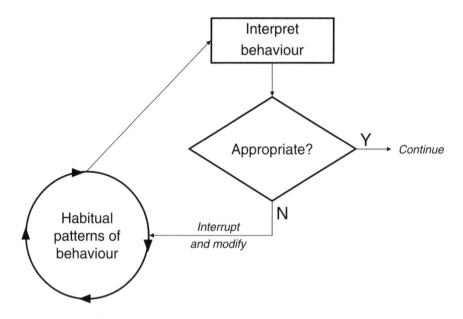

Figure 7.5   Achieving appropriate behavioural flexibility

3.   APPROPRIATELY EXPRESS EMOTIONS

Armed with an internal understanding of those inner feelings and emotions that drive behaviour, the next step in developing emotional literacy is to learn how to express emotions appropriately so other people are able to understand clearly, and so the emotions can be channelled positively rather than ignored or left to fester from within. The following components are required for this: goal-directedness and emotional self-control, personal openness and emotional honesty, assertiveness and conflict-handling, optimism, and constructive discontent. Each of these is detailed below.

Appropriately expressing emotions is not just about expressing positive emotions that lift self and others to see the possibilities that lie ahead. Emotions such as anger, disappointment, frustration and despair also need to be appropriately expressed. In the closest of relationships such emotions are easily expressed and therefore can be dealt with and actually serve to make the relationship alive and real. Skilful two-way communication of 'hot' emotions can have the same effect in business relationships.

The Greek philosopher Aristotle (384–322 BC) writing in 350 BC was already commenting on the difficulties of being emotionally intelligent when it comes to expressing feelings of anger. He said 'Anyone can become angry – that is easy. But to be angry with the right person, to the right degree, at the right time, for the right purpose, and in the right way – this is not easy.'

Goal directedness and emotional self-control

The first step in this process is a feature of emotional literacy typically labelled as 'goal directedness' which represents initiative, and a willingness and readiness to act towards the achievement of long-term goals. For many people, it is much easier to keep emotional thoughts and feelings inside and choose not to divulge them to others rather than to express them appropriately. Expressing emotions in a way that they can be heard positively takes skill and in some cases bravery. Sometimes the motivation to take this step is only for long-term rather than short-term gain. The emotionally literate person recognizes where they need to be willing and ready to appropriately express emotions even if the short-term effect is stressful or takes up valuable time. In contrast, some people are too ready to express their emotions and engage in inappropriate emotional 'dumping' – this is either done intentionally and without personal integrity, or naïvely. Whatever the cause, the right balance between expressing and withholding emotions needs to be found, as shown in Figure 7.6. The ability to find this balanced position is another dimension of emotional intelligence, usually labelled 'emotional expression and emotional self-control'.

Personal openness and emotional honesty

Closely linked to both goal directedness and emotional expression and control is the issue of personal openness and emotional honesty. Dr Samuel Johnson (1709–1784) is

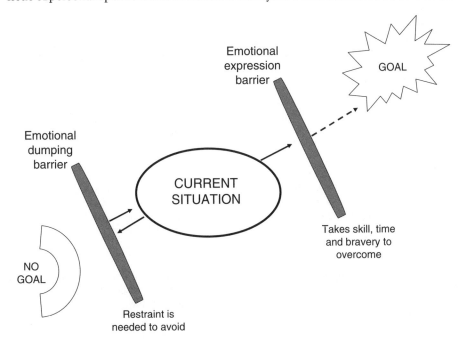

Figure 7.6   Emotional expression and self-control

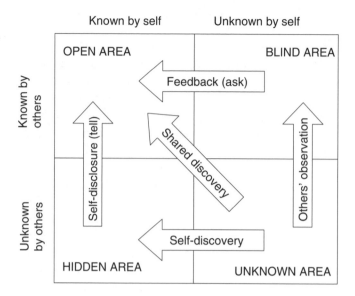

Figure 7.7   Johari Window – adapted from Luft and Ingham , 1955

Table 7.2   Explaining the Johari Window (from Luft and Ingham, 1955)

Open area

The open area is that part of our conscious self, our attitudes, behaviour, motivation, values, way of life of which we are aware and which is known to others. We move within this area with freedom. We are 'open books'.

Hidden area

Our hidden area cannot be known to others unless we disclose it. There is that which we freely keep within ourselves, and that which we retain out of fear. The degree to which we share ourselves with others (disclosure) is the degree to which we can be known.

Blind area

There are things about ourselves which we do not know, but that others can see more clearly; or things we imagine to be true of ourselves for a variety of reasons but that others do not see at all. When others say what they see (feedback) in a supportive, responsible way and we are able to hear it, in that way we are able to test the reality of who we are and are able to grow.

Unknown area

We are more rich and complex than that which we and others know, but from time to time something happens – is felt, read, heard, dreamed – something from our unconscious is revealed. Then we 'know' what we have never known before. This discovery of the unknown can be by self, by others or shared.

It is through disclosure, feedback and discovery that our *open* area is expanded and that we gain access to the potential within us represented by the *unknown* area.

quoted as saying 'A man, Sir, should keep his friendships in constant repair.' Relationships with others, be they close personal relationships or business/professional associations, need to be maintained. The concept that 'to have a friend you need to be a friend' applies to a myriad of situations. One way to achieve this is for people to be open and emotionally honest with the people they interact with, so building a greater understanding and a closer bond that will support the relationship in future.

One popular model for helping individuals handle disclosure about themselves and feedback from others is the four-segment Johari Window, named after Joseph Luft and Harry Ingham who developed the model in the 1950s. The Johari Window is illustrated in Figure 7.7 with explanatory notes in Table 7.2. The figure indicates a number of strategies to expand the 'open area' in which knowledge of self by oneself and others is maximized.

There is clearly a risk in being open with people for the first time. The person you share information with may choose to see you as 'Not OK' in this situation. Caution is needed, combined with intuition about the other person. Some significant people will not be emotionally literate, but they may be organizationally powerful. They are unlikely to be the right people on which to start practising greater emotional honesty. Trust is central to moving forward, both the ability to trust others and the ability to be trustworthy.

Of course, emotional honesty and openness applies equally to sharing difficult emotions and positive ones, to sharing why you have a problem with the behaviour of another person, being prepared to give, and to receive constructive criticism not just praise.

Assertiveness and conflict handling

Assertiveness requires a combined concern for one's own needs and the needs of the other party. People who find it difficult to assert their rights usually have adopted a life position where one party is seen as 'Not OK'; either themselves or others.

A very useful technique for people to use to develop appropriate assertiveness is the 'I' statement as promoted by The Conflict Resolution Network of Australia (see www.crnhq.org). Using an 'I' statement a person can communicate clearly their perception of and feelings about a situation without attacking, blaming or hurting the other person. This opens a discussion without eliciting defensiveness from the other person and gives the best opportunity for a meaningful discussion that will lead to a resolution of any issues.

An 'I' statement has three parts: an objective description of the action, a statement of the feeling the action causes without any blame and a statement of the preferred outcome, for example:

When changes to our plans have been finalized before I have a chance to contribute, *I feel* angry. *What I'd like in future is* to have more involvement in the decision-making process.

Conflict between people is an inevitable part of life. It may be appropriate to avoid a conflict from time to time ('to win the war not the battle') or to force your ideas on another person (for example, where safety is concerned), but an approach to conflict where every party wins something of value to them is necessary to build long-term relationships.

Contemporary attitudes to conflict view it as neither positive nor negative but just as something that is; an opportunity to be made the most of. Resolving conflict is rarely about who is right; it is about acknowledgement and appreciation of differences and achievement of the positive benefits that are there for the skilful to realize. Some of the positive aspects of conflict are shown in Figure 7.8.

Figure 7.8   Potential positive outcomes of conflict

Table 7.3 brings together the Transactional Analysis Life Positions, the ritualistic reactions of the 'reptilian' part of the Triune Brain, conflict handling modes and the need to separate issues and behaviour from personal judgements. This model shows the optimal approach to behaviour in conflict, in contrast with the more instinctive but less effective approaches.

Optimism

One way of dealing with conflict, particularly with people within an existing relationship, is through the use of positive humour. Earlier in this chapter it was highlighted that the part of the human brain that is the emotional centre (the limbic

Table 7.3   Behaviour in conflict

Transactional Analysis	Triune Brain	Conflict handling	Outcome	Resulting behaviour
I'm OK, You're not OK	Fight (aggressive)	I win, You lose	Hard on the person, Hard on the issue	Ineffective
I'm not OK, You're not OK	Flight (submissive)	I lose, You lose	Soft on the person, Soft on the issue	Ineffective
I'm OK, You're OK	**Flow (assertive)**	**I win, You win**	**Soft on the person, Hard on the issue**	**Effective**

system) is an 'open loop' relying on external stimuli for regulation. This simply means that the emotions of other people affect our emotions and therefore our physiology. This is easily illustrated by imagining the effect on you emotionally when someone you care about is openly distressed; the effect is both mental and physical. Barsade and colleagues at Yale University have found that some emotions are spread with greater ease than others through what scientists call 'interpersonal limbic regulation'. The quickest transfers are emotions related to cheerfulness and warmth, with smiles and laughter being literally contagious.

It follows then that enthusiasm and optimism accompanied by emotional signals such as smiles and laughter are key dimensions of emotional literacy. Whilst it may be possible for some people to fake a smile in some circumstances, it is almost impossible for human beings to fake laughter that is perceived as genuine by others. This is not to say that emotionally literate people tell lots of jokes. The emotion that makes the difference is the genuine pleasure related to a situation that matters. The laughter associated with the punch-line to a joke rarely achieves this.

Constructive discontent

A key element of emotional literacy is what some authors label 'constructive discontent'. As the name suggests, this is the ability to discover and use human discontent for a constructive, positive purpose. It is about harnessing the power of emotions that would be negative if left unexpressed, and turning them into something positive.

In a context of '*I'm OK, you're OK*', the power of constructive discontent holds no bounds. Alternatively stated with a quotation from the chewing-gum industrialist

William Wrigley, Jr (1861–1932), 'When two people in business always agree, one of them is unnecessary'. This aspect of emotional literacy is particularly important in group working and is discussed further in Chapter 8.

4.   HANDLE EMOTIONS

Given the ability to recognize, understand and appropriately express emotions, the final step is to develop the tools to be able to handle emotions – of self and others on a continuing basis. Some key dimensions of emotional literacy are specifically relevant to this step, including intentionality, emotional resilience, interdependence and attention to life quality issues.

Intentionality or impulse control

Firstly, some authors refer to a dimension they label 'intentionality', which is about impulse control and delayed gratification. The word 'intentionality' is derived from the commonly used word 'intention', originally from the Latin to mean 'to stretch forward'. People who display high levels of intentionality are focused on development of themselves, being prepared to take temporary setbacks en route to their goal. Another aspect of this dimension is timing. In the section on appropriately expressing emotions it was suggested that it is always best to express an emotion, but this is best done 'at the right time'. Emotionally literate people are able to judge 'the right time' and wait to express their emotions at this time. Early experiments on delayed gratification involving children and marshmallows illustrate the point well. Is it preferable to have one marshmallow now, or three later? This is not an issue of the children taking a risk as three marshmallows would be available later. The issue is whether impulses can be controlled and whether waiting is possible. People who 'want it all, and want it now' are not displaying high levels of intentionality.

Emotional resilience or stress tolerance

The second pivotal aspect of handling emotions is emotional resilience, often called stress tolerance. Simply put, this is the degree to which people are able to pick themselves up and bounce back when things go badly for them. In relation to life positions, '*I'm OK, you're OK*' is fundamental to emotional resilience. 'I'm OK' is needed for people to hold on to their sense of worth and ability in the face of disappointment or rejection. 'You're OK' is needed to remain hopeful and positive about the future in a world full of other people who cannot be controlled.

Interdependence

Related closely to emotional resilience is the concept of interdependence. Some authors describe interdependence as being the healthy balance between dependence (on other people) and independence (which can make others feel excluded). In his bestselling book *The Seven Habits of Highly Effective People*, Steven Covey described and illustrated interdependence in this way:

> Life is, by nature, highly interdependent. To try to achieve maximum effectiveness through independence is like trying to play tennis with a golf club; the tool is not suited to the reality. Interdependence is a mature and advanced concept and is a choice only independent people can make. Dependent people cannot choose to become interdependent because they don't own enough of themselves.

Reflection on how society has developed in the western world in recent times will illustrate how many relationships, certainly socially, but often too in business have become dependent. This tends to sap energy from at least one party and can represent a life position where a person feels they are 'Not OK' on their own and always need the help of others. The person being relied upon can also develop a 'You're not OK' attitude to the dependence over time. The other extreme is independent, which in recent decades has been a highly valued attribute particularly for business. However, this has downsides where the independent person then struggles to let others into the picture, feeling that 'I'm OK' but 'You're not OK' as you interfere in what I want to do.

Interdependence is not easy to achieve, but is a necessary position for handling emotions where the drive to work with emotional honesty with others is just as strong as the drive to be able to achieve things alone.

General health and quality of life

The final step in handling emotions involves general health and quality of life. It is neither possible nor desirable here to outline best practice for physical, behavioural and emotional health. However, it is clearly difficult for a person to develop the other attributes of emotional literacy if they are over-tired, under-nourished, lacking in exercise, lacking intellectual stimulation or experiencing any of a myriad of other symptoms of suboptimal lifestyle. Developing emotional literacy therefore requires a holistic approach to mind and body where the interconnections between the two are fully recognized and respected.

STAGES OF INDIVIDUAL EMOTIONAL DEVELOPMENT

Having understood the components of emotional literacy, individuals need to know how to develop them.

Many diagnostic tools for assessing emotional literacy are available commercially (see Appendix), and the companies that promote these tools also offer services to help individuals through their journey to greater emotional literacy. Such support typically involves feedback and some element of coaching. In addition, some organizations are proactive in supporting individuals through coaching and mentoring interventions.

For individuals seeking to understand how to develop their own emotional literacy, it is important to understand the basic stages that humans experience as emotions develop, as shown in Figure 7.9. These are derived from Claude Steiner's book *Emotional Literacy: Intelligence with a Heart,* and have been developed as a result of many years of experience working with people to develop emotional literacy. Steiner, as a psychologist and therapist, works with some people who are deeply emotionally illiterate, at the start of the spectrum, and who are numb to emotions. He also regularly works with people who by all other measures are 'successful' in business or personal terms, but where their success achieved through traditional intellect, money or other sources of external power has become stifled by their lack of emotional literacy and personal power. For many people, the verbal barrier of Figure 7.9 (also shown as the emotional expression barrier in Figure 7.6) remains to be overcome. Until an individual can describe specifically what emotions they are presently experiencing, they cannot move forward to understanding causes of their own emotions and into understanding others: without this there can be no meaningful control; emotions will influence either positively or negatively and people will succeed, or not, by accident.

To want to overcome this verbal barrier, people must believe that appropriate expression and handling of emotions is central to personal effectiveness in any situation.

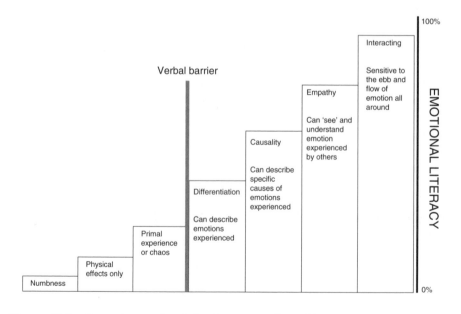

Figure 7.9   Stages in emotional development (adapted from Steiner)

In the final analysis, the choice to become more emotionally literate lies with each individual. For those who make the choice, there are many sources of help and support available. For those in any position of leadership, whether in a family, a social group or a workplace, Goleman's words in *Primal Leadership* may strike a chord and provide a challenge to take some further development steps: 'No creature can fly with just one wing. Gifted leadership occurs when heart and head – feeling and thought – meet. These are the two wings that allow a leader to soar.'

Developing emotional literacy in individuals is powerful and can have a direct effect on the ability to make good decisions in uncertain situations. Risk management in organizations, however, is not typically controlled by an individual, but needs to be a collective effort. Accordingly, there is an imperative to build emotionally literate groups to prevent the emotions of the collective becoming a barrier to effective decision making. Chapter 8 explores this area of group emotional literacy.

Emotional Literacy for Groups

In turning the focus of attention to the emotional literacy of groups, it is important to remember that groups, that is collections of individuals, operate at a number of levels as defined in Chapter 2. This pointed out that the characteristic of any group, be it risk attitude or level of emotional literacy, is not merely the sum or the average of the component parts. However, just as the risk attitude of a group is fundamentally influenced by the risk attitudes of the individuals making up the group, the emotional literacy of any group will be directly affected by the emotional literacy of the members of that group.

In considering groups, the primary focus of this chapter is the small working team, that is a collection of individuals who are working together for a common purpose. This may be a project team at work or in a community setting, or a specialist team working together in a functional department. Similarly the small working team may be a company board or senior management team. Whilst the risk attitude of an organization will be affected by issues relating to the deep-rooted culture of the company itself and the sector and national context, as discussed in Chapter 5, it is also a fact that the daily decisions in an organization can be significantly affected by the risk attitudes of the members of the senior management team.

As previously discussed, whatever the goals of individuals may be, success happens (or fails to happen) in a social context. The open loop nature of the emotional centre of the human brain means that for emotional stability, people rely on connections with other people. The more positive these connections are, the more emotionally stable each individual will be. It is obvious therefore that any group of people, whether a family group, a project team, a social group or any sort of larger organization, will have a better chance of harnessing the emotional energy within the group for positive benefit if the members are emotionally literate as individuals.

Regarding decision-making and making choices in risky situations in particular, the emotional state of the group will get in the way of the process if it is not recognized, understood, appropriately expressed and managed. In the context of risk management, it is critical to identify and deal with those 'emotions that matter', namely those feelings that will prevent the group from achieving the best solution if they are left unacknowledged or unmanaged.

Where at least some of the powerful members of a group are emotionally literate as individuals, it is relatively easy to build a culture within the group where feelings are openly discussed and handled in a way that protects the person involved. With skilful handling, the development of emotional literacy across the whole group can then move quickly as a virtuous cycle is generated. Behaviour breeds behaviour. The effect on the group will be positive if behaviour is positive, encouraging and supportive, if the prevailing culture within the group is one where people are 'hard on the issue and soft on the person', if the link between emotional literacy and success can be established, and if emotionally damaging behaviours are rejected by the group. The group will soon know themselves well enough that they don't get in the way of their decision-making processes.

Conversely, the way forward for the group will be more difficult if the powerful members of a group are the sorts of people who believe that emotional literacy is mutually exclusive with business acumen, that emotions are private and should be kept tightly reined in, or that feelings are irrational and have no place alongside logical decision-making.

So far it is clear that emotion has a direct effect on risk management and can be managed. Individuals must accept the challenge to analyse and enhance their own emotional literacy. Accepting this challenge for oneself then makes us fit for the purpose of promoting emotional literacy and helping others in the groups and teams in which we work and play.

COMPONENT PARTS OF GROUP EMOTIONAL LITERACY

There has been little specific research into the emotional literacy of groups. Most published work takes the dimensions of emotional literacy as applied to individuals and applies these to groups. All of the elements of emotional literacy examined in Chapter 7 are relevant to groups since they affect the constituent individuals within the group, but some factors are more specifically relevant to understanding how the emotional literacy of groups affects risk attitudes. These are listed in Table 8.1, and discussed below under the four major elements of emotional literacy, as in Chapter 7, namely:

1. recognize emotions

2. understand emotions

3. appropriately express emotions, and

4. handle emotions.

Table 8.1   Relevant diagnostic elements of emotional literacy for groups

1. Recognize emotions
- Group 'self'-awareness
- Organizational awareness

2. Understand emotions
- Relative regard

3. Appropriately express emotions
- Personal openness and emotional honesty
- Assertiveness and conflict handling

4. Handle emotions
- Intentionality/impulse control
- Emotional resilience/stress tolerance

1.   RECOGNIZE EMOTIONS

Group 'self'-awareness

It is important for groups to recognize any habitual, rigid patterns of behaviour that have become established as the norm. As previously described, habitual behaviour has many positive aspects: it allows people to flow and take decisions easily and without stress. There can also, however, be a number of detrimental effects of habits adopted by a group.

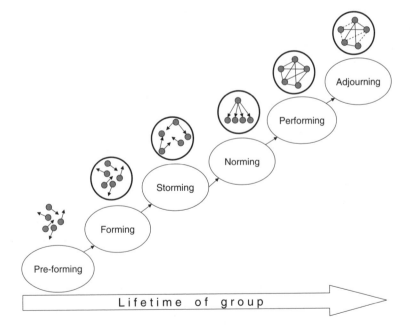

Figure 8.1   Stages in group development (after Tuckman)

In 1965, Bruce Tuckman introduced his model for group development highlighting the stages a group passes through to become a 'performing' team, as illustrated in Figure 8.1. In the 'norming' stage, Tuckman explained how groups have found a way for the individual members to work together without negative conflict, but they have not yet reached a level of maturity where they are able to express themselves and harness the positive aspects of disagreements. Experience has shown that many groups become 'stuck' at the norming stage where they are having fun together and working efficiently on the tasks that they are set, including making decisions in uncertain situations; however, they are not challenging each other and using constructive discontent to push the boundaries that would make them effective as well as efficient.

Habitual behaviour within groups is closely linked to the heuristics which affect group behaviour in general and group risk attitudes in particular as described in Chapter 5. Heuristics work at a subconscious level and in a systematic way to short-cut the mental process. They can be very useful rules of thumb, but can also bias decision-making in an unwanted way if left unrecognized and unexamined.

Groups that demonstrate habitual behaviours, such as always adopting a risk-seeking attitude, may be adopting the 'cultural conformity' heuristic – making decisions that match the perceived expectation of the organization or cultural norm. Alternatively the group may be locked into 'groupthink' where the members of a cohesive group choose to preserve harmony and not challenge the status quo. In such situations, it may be that there are few strong emotions associated with adopting the usual risk attitude, where the security of a habitualized approach can be compelling, but also blinding. In contrast, however, if strong emotions are felt by individual members but not expressed this can be deeply ineffective, both in the short term if the group decision did not take into account all relevant factors, and in the longer term if the burying of the emotion was left unresolved. If strong emotions about the issue being discussed or about other members of the group are appropriately recognized, understood and expressed, there is a chance for different behaviours to be displayed and a modified risk attitude to be adopted if appropriate. An example might be where a group member has had a previous encounter with a client and no trust exists between the two parties. The group may choose to adopt a more risk-averse stance with the client given this knowledge, or to build in safeguards to counter the chance that the client cannot be trusted this time. Conversely, the group may choose not to adapt their tactics in the light of this information, but can nevertheless be empathetic to the group member and willing to help them through their personal difficulty.

It is therefore important for groups to find a way of reflecting on their current normalized patterns and deciding whether they are optimal. If the group has no mechanism for dealing with the emotions of the individual members it is likely to be operating sub-optimally.

Organizational awareness

This is one of the elements of emotional literacy that plays a role at both an individual and group level, determining how social relationships are managed. Awareness of cultural, political or sociological aspects of an organization's context is the first step towards effective management within that context. Techniques such as PESTLE analysis are commonly used to prompt research into and understanding of organizational context (see Figure 8.2). Similarly, stakeholder analysis can be helpful, using a simple model to consider the power and interest of key individuals and groups who can help or hinder progress.

Type of factor	External examples	Internal examples
P = Political	Central or local government	Within the business – interplay of power and motivation
E = Economic	Sensitivities to macro economic variations, e.g. taxation or interest rates	Financial considerations such as profitability, cash-flow or return on investment
S = Sociological	Expectations or attitudes of society at large National cultural issues	Organizational cultural issues Attitudes to change
T = Technological	Changing technological capability and expectations	Attitudes to technological change
L = Legal	Statutory requirements and legal obligations	Local application of statutory requirements Attitudes to legal obligations
E = Ecological (environmental)	Changing legislation and attitudes to issues such as renewable energy, future disposal	Local attitudes to ecological issues

Figure 8.2   PESTLE analysis

Having carried out this first step to gain a rational awareness, the second step is to understand how the group feels about the situation, what emotions are held and whether they matter. If this is not done, any strong emotions which are felt but left unmanaged will deflect attention from successful achievement of the group goal whatever that may be.

2.   UNDERSTANDING EMOTIONS

When a group has been able to recognize that emotions are affecting the shared decision-making process, they then need to understand those emotions as a precursor to expressing them appropriately.

In a group situation, it is important to be able to understand the difference between emotions that are personal to an individual, and emotions that are shared by a larger number of people. All individuals are important, but the route for exploring a personal emotion that is getting in the way may not be in the group context. Developing group emotional literacy should be managed so it does not turn into group therapy. Emotions shared by a number of people, however, are very likely to affect risk attitudes and decision-making and therefore they need to be understood so they can be managed for positive effect.

Relative regard

The value of relative regard is essential for development of group emotional literacy. Each individual in the group needs to feel that they are 'OK' and are worthy of being heard, and that others are 'OK' and can be trusted to empathize and support them.

Understanding emotions in a group situation relies on each individual being able to see the situation through the eyes of others and then being able to rationalize this data and see a clear path forward that respects how others are thinking and feeling. This is easy to say but not always easy to do, as our own emotions often get in the way of understanding and respecting another who sees the world differently. In a group context the need for relative regard is fundamental and critical to effectiveness.

3.   APPROPRIATELY EXPRESSING EMOTIONS

Personal openness, emotional honesty and assertiveness

In Chapter 5, the effects of national cultural differences on risk attitudes were discussed, focusing on the work of Hofstede in defining the distinguishing dimensions of a national culture. This is also directly relevant to expressing emotions in groups.

Hofstede's Power Distance dimension of national culture deals with the extent to which a society sees inequality between people and a hierarchical structure to society as a necessary evil, or a fundamental basis for societal order. Table 5.1 shows the power distance index (PDI) for the countries studied by Hofstede. In a country with a high PDI, inequalities are expected and desired by the less powerful. In a country with a low PDI, inequalities are barely tolerated, and are only done so for the purposes of basic order, for example in government.

The significance of this for expressing emotions is that in a culture with a higher PDI, the acceptance and respect for superiors limit the extent to which people feel they are free to express their views and emotions, whereas in a culture with a lower PDI, it is acceptable and desirable to question authority. It is much easier for communication to be open and two-way in a group that has a low power distance index.

Linked to this research is the work of Edward Hall on high-context and low-context cultures. In a high-context culture the meaning of words and actions are derived and contextualized from the environment. Communication is heavily implicit and such cultures rely on intuition, reflection and sensory perception of issues. Korea and Middle Eastern countries are typically high context. In contrast, low-context cultures rely on explicit verbal communication to convey meaning. In such cultures the content of the communication is far more important than the means of delivery of the message. Whilst non-verbal communication inevitably plays a part it has less of an impact than the words themselves. Scandinavian countries are typically low context.

Whilst there is no definitive correlation between Hofstede's power distance and Hall's high/low context, cultures with a higher PDI appear likely to be higher context than those with low PDI.

The consequences for the emotional literacy of individuals and groups are significant, since appropriate expression of emotion will mean different things to different people. In some cultures, appropriate expression will be subtle and non-verbal relying on the intuition of other group members to recognize and understand it. In other cultures, appropriate expression will be explicit and verbal, this time relying on the ability of the other group members to be able to deal with this direct approach. In a multicultural team the value of understanding other people at an individual level cannot be over-stated if communication and decision-making are to be effective.

It is perhaps significant that the development and popularization of emotional literacy has taken place in countries with cultures that tend to be lower power distance and lower-context. Chapter 7 showed that working with individuals to build emotional literacy has relied on people being able to cross the 'verbal barrier' and develop an ability to talk about emotions to a trusted other person. It has been demonstrated that development only occurs when people find a way of talking about their emotions in an appropriate way.

In a group situation the verbal barrier is perhaps even higher with greater levels of risk for individuals to disclose feelings in a group context. Group emotional literacy, however, still depends on emotional expression for development.

4.   HANDLING EMOTIONS

Intentionality/impulse control

At its most basic level, handling emotions depends on deciding what emotions *matter* – which emotions can take the group forward towards their goal, and which will detract from the goal.

Recognizing, understanding and appropriately expressing emotions within the group will build trust and effectiveness. However, in just the same way that individuals need to choose the right moment to express emotions to others, groups also need to be able to make judgements about 'the right time and place' and deal with emotions so that the ones that impact on goals are heard, and the ones that don't are dealt with within the group. For example, a group may collectively feel trepidation about a project they are engaged in because no one is very experienced in the field and because they feel they have a point to prove to their management. It would be appropriate for the group to confront their feelings of trepidation, understand where they come from and work together to deal with them. It would be inappropriate to share their trepidation with anyone who may pass on the information to the management team. Discussing issues privately within a group and then not passing the information freely on to others requires intentionality – an intention to achieve the goal rather than be side-tracked by issues on the way.

Resilience/stress tolerance

The ability for a group to pick themselves up and bounce back when things go badly for them is central to effectiveness and can be developed. In just the same way that an individual's self-esteem and personal power can go into a negative (vicious) cycle or a positive (virtuous) cycle as their performance reinforces their internal image, the same is true for groups. Some groups are not resilient and things that go badly have a deep effect on the group esteem as well as on individual members of a group. Conversely, other groups are robust and sometimes arrogant, with little external influence having an effect.

The reality is that neither type of group is emotionally literate. The emotionally literate group is resilient and tenacious, but reaches this position after looking honestly at the truth of the situation, including how individuals feel.

Sometimes a safe place for a group to start to explore emotions is following a set-back. Understanding what people feel about the situation can help both the group effort and the individuals themselves.

THE ROLE OF LEADERSHIP

The development of emotional literacy for an individual is challenging enough and typically relies on that person having good support from others around them. The development of emotionally literate groups is a further step requiring positive intent, tenacity and skill. The challenge calls for leadership of the highest order to act as a catalyst for the group and to be a role model going forward to a more emotionally literate future.

Whilst the whole field of leadership is extensively covered in the literature, there are some aspects of leadership that are relevant to emotionally literate groups, and these are explored below.

OBJECTIVE SETTING

Emotional literacy insists that awareness must precede action. This is supported by Covey who asserts that 'private victories precede public victories', emphasizing the need for people and groups first to understand themselves, their feelings and motivations before making decisions and influencing others.

Since both risks and attitudes are defined in terms of objectives, it is not possible for a group to act effectively unless those objectives are clearly defined and agreed by all key stakeholders. One major role of leadership in projects, teams and organizations is to ensure that objectives are set in an emotionally literate way. This requires allowing the group first to reflect upon and discuss what its automatic response would be to the risks associated with the situation, and determining the possible effect on achievement of objectives. With time, relative regard and intentionality in place, the group could begin a rich discussion about how to modify their subconscious risk attitude in order to set appropriate and achievable objectives.

GROUP MOTIVATION

The term 'alignment' is often used to describe leading a group of people towards a common goal, drawing on a magnet metaphor indicating the need to get all the constituent parts pointing in the right direction. Rational descriptions of goals, objectives or project success criteria may be somewhat bland, but the organization expects that people will align to them and be motivated to achieve them.

Considering this analogy in terms of the Triune Brain explained in Chapter 7, rational language speaks to the neo-cortex which is the logical centre of the brain, and completely bypasses the part of the brain concerned with emotion and feeling. As a result, rational language does not usually engender passion and commitment. Understanding this, US leadership expert Warren Bennis suggests that effective groups should work on 'attuning' rather than 'aligning'. For musical instruments, attuning describes the process of bringing harmony by achieving a resonance. The emotional intelligence equivalent means accessing what people feel about the goal as a means of harnessing a collective energy and passion about moving towards it.

Psychologist Lou Tice says that 'all meaningful and lasting change starts on the inside and works its way out', and this is true for groups as well as individuals. So if a group chooses to modify its natural risk attitudes in a particular situation, this will only be effective if the group is attuned to the objective with their heart as well as their head.

CULTURAL FLUENCY

The effects of national cultural differences on risk attitudes and on emotional literacy cannot be ignored, and multicultural groups fail to understand the effect of the cultural mix at their peril. Clearly there is a major role for leadership to ensure that this is addressed in the groups for which they are responsible.

For example using the results from the Hofstede research (see Figure 5.3) the following national cultural stereotypes might be exhibited by a group made up of individuals from Norway, Malaysia and France who have been brought together within their organization to manage the introduction of a new technology into a new market:

- The Norwegians would tend to be comfortable with ambiguity, intolerant of inequalities and very focused on verbal rather than non-verbal communication.

- The Malaysians would similarly tend to be comfortable with ambiguity but in contrast see inequalities in society as being essential and be high context with non-verbal communication being more important than the words spoken.

- The French would tend to be uncomfortable with ambiguity and would prefer a hierarchy of power within society. Verbal and non-verbal communication would play an equal part.

If these cultural factors were left unmanaged, there would be a high chance that communication would be ineffective and the group might have no mechanism for determining an appropriate attitude to the uncertainties inherent in their situation. Decision-making would be at best slow and at worst non-inclusive, with the most powerful group member(s) imposing their preferences on the group.

The purpose of this example is not to focus particularly on these three nations, but to demonstrate that cross-cultural working is mostly complex and full of hidden dangers that are directly applicable to risk attitudes and risk management, and that understanding national cultural differences can help manage these challenges. This could be achieved by a group leader who ensured that the group focused on their goal while allowing each person to communicate their feelings about the goal and the associated risks. This would create shared understanding and permit the group to choose a way forward with an agreed group risk attitude for the situation.

USE OF POWER

Every member of a group contributes to the overall degree of emotional literacy of the group, but the group leader has a particularly influential position, since emotions are contagious and behaviour breeds behaviour. A skilful leader will balance objective setting and decision-making with attention to the relationships between group members. In contrast, leaders can wreak havoc by displaying counter-productive emotions, allowing negative competition to develop within the group, or ridiculing attempts for greater communication at an emotional level.

The different sources of power that leaders can exercise have been discussed earlier, and these can have a major influence on the emotional literacy of the group. The ideal situation is clearly where the official group leader (that is the person with legitimate and reward/coercion power) is emotionally literate. The next best situation is where the group leader themself may not be emotionally literate, but is open to the concept and is prepared to allow another group member to lead this aspect of the group's development and work, based on their referent or expert power.

MEETING BEHAVIOURS

Given that a large percentage of group work is conducted in a meeting setting, one of the main responsibilities of the leader is to work to ensure that meetings are positive and supportive of the group's emotional development aims.

Communication in group situations has a direct effect on success. Much time in organizations tends to be spent in formal meetings: these can be inspiring gatherings that achieve much, but the reverse is experienced too often. Hendrie Weisinger suggests that team communication in meetings can be fostered by:

- using and encouraging self-disclosure, sharing thoughts and feelings relating directly to the situation being discussed;

- practising and encouraging dynamic listening, using restatement, reality checking and building on replies;

- engaging in problem-solving, using solution-focused thinking;

- using assertiveness and constructive criticism, since emotionally literate groups welcome honest exchange and robust debate focused on the issue not the individuals in the team.

This approach is supported by research conducted by Cary Chernis into emotional intelligence in organizations. He recommends handing out a list of 'process norms' alongside the agenda at the beginning of a meeting, to remind group members of their behavioural responsibilities as well as the work to be done. These process norms might include:

- keeping on track;

- encouraging the input of others;

- use of clarification and summary to make sure there is a shared understanding;

- listening and building on what others say.

This requires the leader of the group to be sufficiently emotionally aware and
confident to take this approach. Such leadership behaviour is essential if emotional
development within a group is to be consistent and progressive.

USE OF LANGUAGE

Neuro-Linguistic Programming (NLP) has become popularized in recent years. It was
developed initially by Richard Bandler and John Grinder in the early 1970s, who set out
to identify the patterns used by outstanding therapists who achieved excellent results
with clients. One aspect of NLP involves building rapport with others, which is a key
element of emotional literacy of direct relevance to group working.

Individuals represent information internally through their basic senses, that is in
pictures (visual), sounds (auditory), feelings (kinaesthetic), taste (gustatory) and smell
(olfactory). This manifests itself in the language people use, for example some people
will automatically say 'that looks good to me', others will say 'sounds right' and yet
others will say 'that feels good'. They all mean the same thing, that the situation is
good, but the representational system they use to communicate is different. Excellent
communicators, often instinctively, recognize the representational systems preferred
by others and work with them. They use different representational systems to include
and reach each member of the group, and give each person an opportunity to relate to
and engage with the message.

Relating NLP to risk attitudes, each group member will have their own mental map
of each uncertain situation that exists. The skilful leader will enable each member of
the group to verbalize their understanding of the situation. The sensory language that
different people use will vary and this may result in the expression of their risk attitude
also varying. Group members may actually agree, for example, that something is a
good opportunity, but counter this with different attitudes to the actions that should
be taken next. This could lead to group members failing to understand how each other
is feeling about the uncertainty, for example, believing that they are disagreeing when
in fact they have considerable common ground. A skilful leader will recognize this and
be able to use a range of sensory language to build rapport and understanding within
the group.

Another area where the group leader should be aware of the effect of language is
the use of humour. Sometimes this can mask sarcasm, prejudice or personal criticism.
Chapter 7 outlined the importance of optimism as part of the development of

emotional literacy and the importance of laughter in building genuine relationships with others and building attitudes that see the future in a positive, opportunity-laden light. Unfortunately, not all types of humour achieve this, with some appearing to be funny in the short term but actually only being destructive to development of effective emotionally literate groups in the longer term. Negative humour destroys trust and the relative regard required for people to openly state their viewpoints, and damages respect within the group. Effective leaders recognize this and make sure that this type of language is known to be unacceptable.

GOING FORWARD

The value of developing emotional literacy within groups at all levels is undeniable. This is true in business, for project teams, departments, divisions and organizations as a whole. It is also true outside work, in families, communities, clubs and social settings. While the emotional literacy of constituent individuals is a major contributor to the emotional literacy of the groups to which they belong, there are a number of group-specific factors to be considered. Some of these require attention by the group working together and others are the particular responsibility of the group leader.

Whether at individual or group level, however, emotional literacy does not just happen. Chapters 7 and 8 have outlined the component parts of emotional literacy for both individuals and groups in order to promote awareness of the issues to be addressed. But awareness must be followed by action, in order to gain the benefits of emotionally literate teams and groups.

This is clearly important to individuals and organizations for a number of reasons, since emotions have a significant effect across the business environment, both positively and negatively. There is, however, a particular application to the understanding and management of risk attitudes. Part 2 developed a framework describing risk attitudes at both individual and group levels, and Part 3 has detailed the components of emotional literacy. These can now be brought together to explore ways in which application of emotional literacy can allow risk attitudes to be understood and managed, leading to more effective management of risk wherever it is found. Part 4 presents such an approach, applying the principles of emotional literacy directly to risk attitudes.

Implementation Issues

CHAPTER 9

Applying Emotional Literacy to Risk Attitudes

Having described the problem with risk management effectiveness and the role of human factors as a Critical Success Factor, a number of issues arise. Central to all these is the interaction between people and uncertainty, crystallized in their risk attitude – the chosen response to significant uncertainty. Risk attitudes are displayed by both individuals and groups, and there are many influences on these, both open and hidden. People adopt an attitude to each risky situation that reflects their perception of the degree to which the uncertainty matters to them, and their emotional feelings towards the uncertainty.

Risk attitudes are usually adopted subconsciously, the exception being when the person or group involved consciously decides to over-ride their automatic response because they want to understand the situation more clearly, and make an appropriate rather than automatic choice.

Free-flowing subconscious behaviour can be good in that it allows people to make good decisions in uncertain situations quickly and without effort. For example a person who tends to be risk-averse in uncertain situations affecting personal safety would not hesitate to leave a building that was burning down rather than delay to collect personal possessions. It can also be bad if the habitual behaviour is ineffective and continually results in sub-optimal decisions being made. An example here might be a person whose subconscious risk attitude is risk-averse who, faced with an opportunity in a business with a high chance of occurrence, would automatically say no, focusing only on the reasons why the chance may not work out for them.

As discussed in previous chapters, there are many factors that affect an individual's natural, subconscious risk attitude in a given situation (see Chapter 4). For groups of people, an even greater number of factors come into play (Chapter 5). Nevertheless both individuals and groups, faced with an uncertain situation, will adopt a risk attitude that falls somewhere on the risk attitude spectrum shown as Figure 9.1. As outlined in Chapter 2, each person is a complex individual whose attitudes defy simple categorization; nevertheless the risk attitude spectrum is a useful tool to demonstrate the potential range of risk attitudes that could be adopted, and to focus attention on one's own habitual behaviour when faced with a risky situation.

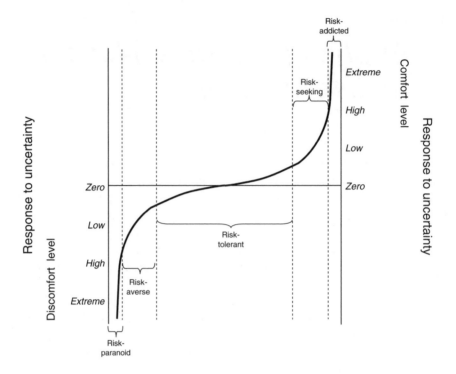

Figure 9.1   Spectrum of risk attitudes

To manage risk attitudes it important to understand how an initial unmanaged risk attitude is adopted, recognizing that this is a subconscious process. There appear to be two distinct alternatives for how a particular individual or group might respond subconsciously to an uncertain situation, and definitive evidence does not currently exist to determine which might be a more accurate reflection of reality:

- The first possibility is that a person or group has a particular default position on the risk attitude spectrum from which they always start, and then they subconsciously adjust from this depending on the influence of perceptual factors or heuristics. This is illustrated in Figure 9.2, which shows an individual who always starts as slightly risk-averse, but who can be moved to be either risk-tolerant or more risk-averse by the effect of perception and/or heuristics. Similarly a group is shown which is generally quite risk-seeking, but which can be influenced to be either more or less so.

- An alternative is that the starting position on the risk attitude spectrum taken by an individual or group is variable, depending on the specific characteristics of the uncertain situation, but that this position is adopted without conscious thought, as shown in Figure 9.3, where a given individual

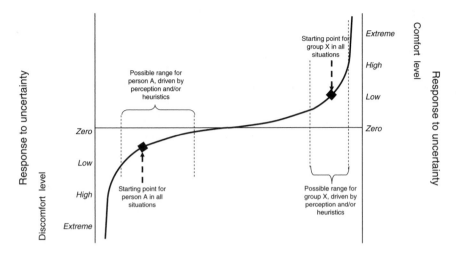

Figure 9.2   Default initial risk attitude

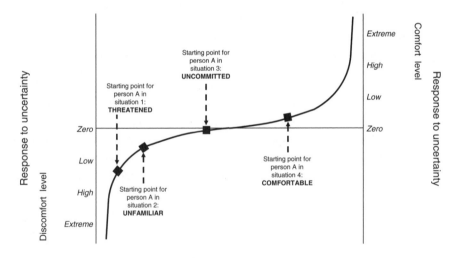

Figure 9.3   Situational initial risk attitude

might adopt differing initial risk attitudes depending on their subconscious perception of the situation.

In time, scientific research may be able to distinguish between these two positions, or to demonstrate some other option, but currently it is not possible to determine how risk attitudes are initially adopted by individuals and groups.

Irrespective of precisely how individuals and groups arrive subconsciously at their initial risk attitude in the light of a given uncertain situation, it remains the case that risk attitude (like all other attitudes) is in fact a choice. However some do not see it as such, describing themselves as 'usually risk-averse' or 'always risk-seeking'. This is because the choice may have become so deeply habitualized that the outcome is largely constant unless there is an extraordinary reason for it to be different. As a result the person or group acts as if they had no choice, simply accepting the attitude which has been adopted subconsciously. This may be described as 'choosing not to choose'. In contrast other individuals and groups have learned to assess each situation internally, and then to choose a risk attitude explicitly, selecting the attitude which is most appropriate to the situation and which offers the best chance of achieving their objectives.

Clearly the emotionally literate approach to this involves both awareness and action, which is likely to be more effective than choosing not to choose and simply adopting whatever risk attitude comes naturally. The first step towards proactively understanding and managing risk attitudes in this way is to develop a strong sense of self-awareness, which is one of fundamental building blocks of emotional literacy.

Self-awareness has a key role in making decisions, to understand what the individual or group is thinking and feeling and how that affects judgement. It also plays a part following each decision, knowing what has just happened, why the decision was taken, how the individual or group feels about it and what would be done differently next time. Self-awareness can be developed, and its importance in determining the quality of decision-making should ensure that it is given considerable attention, so that people are operating more by judgement than luck. High self-awareness enables good judgement, which should produce high-quality decision-making unless one is unlucky. If self-awareness is low, then failure and poor decisions are to be expected, unless one just happens to be lucky and make a good decision.

This relationship between self-awareness and good decision-making is directly relevant to the management of risk attitudes, since individuals and groups cannot hope to adopt appropriate risk attitudes without a high degree of self-awareness.

EMOTIONALLY LITERATE MANAGEMENT OF RISK ATTITUDES

The starting premise for emotionally literate management of risk attitudes is that each individual can over-ride their subconsciously chosen risk attitude in a particular situation if they have a sufficiently strong desire to do so. The motivation will be strongest in situations when it matters, when emotions are either preventing the person from taking a risk that could have a favourable outcome for them, or encouraging them to take a risk unwisely. New thinking patterns must be established which reflect emotional literacy, and which will initially seem uncomfortable and counterintuitive. At first this will need to be a very conscious and deliberate process. As with the development of any skill or habit, with repetition the process will be internalized and become a natural behaviour in itself.

It is clear that emotionally literate individuals form the essential raw material for an emotionally literate group. Just as individuals need to take responsibility for development of their own emotional literacy (in all areas, not just as applied to risk attitudes), so each group will need to consider the issues involved and decide whether and how to apply them. Managing risk attitudes using emotional literacy is not a quick fix that can be applied to every group interaction. As with all things worthwhile, an investment is needed, and one role of the leader is to decide whether for a particular group in a particular context, the investment is justified.

In order to learn how to manage risk attitudes in a group, one has to slow down in order to speed up. To develop group emotional literacy, the group needs first to be self-aware, and that means slowing down, taking time to reflect and discuss as an investment in the future efficiency and effectiveness of the group.

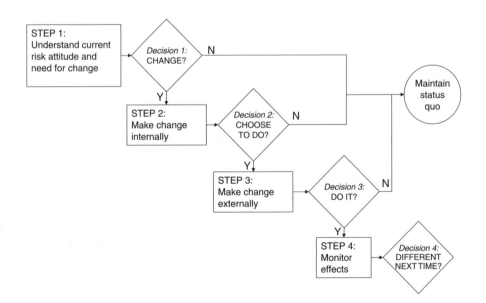

Figure 9.4   Applying emotional literacy to change risk attitude

MAKING THE CHANGE

For both individuals and groups, application of emotional literacy to the understanding and management of risk attitudes requires a deliberate process. This can be summarized in four steps with decision points between each one, as illustrated in Figure 9.4. The process is illustrated in detail in Table 9.1 for each of the four steps, with each step describing the questions that a person or group needs to address in order to:

- analyse their current risk attitude in a particular situation and their motivation to change it;
- prepare themselves for making the change;
- make the change;
- monitor the effects and learn from the experience.

The process is the same for individuals and groups, though some of the steps differ in detail. Table 9.1 is presented as a checklist, and readers should refer back into earlier chapters for explanatory details on each question, or revision of the key concepts and issues associated with each element of the change process. Implementation of this process can be performed by an individual or group working alone, though it may be more effective to use a skilled facilitator able to reflect back and encourage change.

SUMMARY AND FIRST STEPS

Risk attitudes for individuals and groups can be managed once the starting premise – the need for self-awareness – has been embraced. This forms the basis for an essential prerequisite to effective management of risk attitudes at both individual and group levels, namely understanding, which would not be possible without a degree of self-awareness. Although individuals and groups are complex, both internally and in their interrelationships, a structured process as depicted in Table 9.1 can provide a framework for applying the insights of emotional literacy to the management of risk attitudes in an open manner.

There is, however, no quick fix, and those wishing to understand and manage their attitudes to significant uncertainty must be prepared to invest in the process. But this investment promises considerable returns, as individuals and groups learn more about their inherent responses to uncertainty, and develop effective mechanisms for making appropriate adjustments.

Table 9.1   Managing risk attitudes

STEP 1 – UNDERSTAND CURRENT RISK ATTITUDE AND THE NEED FOR CHANGE

Describe and capture in writing:

What is the situation – current reality?
What objectives need to be achieved in this situation?
What are the main risks (threats or opportunities)?
How likely is it that the risks will happen?
Are the possible effects perceived as good, bad or neutral?
Are there obvious actions that can be taken to reduce the threats to an acceptable level?
Are there obvious actions that can be taken to make the opportunities happen?
What perceptual factors might influence assessment of the risks, e.g. level of relevant skills, perception of impact magnitude, degree of perceived control, closeness of the risk in time, potential for direct consequences?
Are individual heuristics having an effect, e.g. availability, representativeness, anchoring and adjustment, confirmation trap?
Are group heuristics having an effect, e.g. cultural conformity, risky shift, groupthink?
What emotions are felt when the risks are considered ?
Do the emotions felt have a physiological effect?
Without any amendment, what risk attitude would be adopted?
Is this an appropriate risk attitude in the situation given the objectives, and if not, what risk attitude might be more appropriate?
What would be the consequences of amending risk attitude in this way – upsides and downsides?
How will feelings differ if another risk attitude is chosen?
Is this good?
Who else will be affected if an amended risk attitude is chosen?
What will be the impact of the choice on objectives, or the objectives of others?

Decision 1 – choose to change risk attitude (yes or no)?

STEP 2 – MAKING THE CHANGE INTERNALLY

Describe and capture in writing:

The situation with the new risk attitude – what does it look and feel like?
What habits need to be amended to move forward to the goal?
What needs to change so that everyone feels 'I'm OK'?
Are people confident in their ability to make this change?
What must people do to get confident and stay confident?
What feelings exist about the others directly involved in the situation – what must change so people feel that 'They are OK'?
Is it necessary to stop judging a person (me or someone else) by their actions?
What needs to happen to stop other people constraining progress?
Whose help is needed for support ?
Who needs to be trusted? Will they be trusted and trustworthy? If not, how will that be dealt with?
What tactics will be adopted to stay resilient if things don't go well?
What tactics will be adopted to keep humility and a sense of perspective if things go very well?
What feelings exist now, both internal thoughts and external effects?

Decision 2 – choose to live out the changed risk attitude (yes or no)?

Continued

Table 9.1   Managing risk attitudes – *concluded*

STEP 3 – MAKING THE CHANGE EXTERNALLY

Write down plans for how the choice will be made:

In what circumstances will the goal be revealed to others, when will it help, when would it be best to control impulses?

How will the goal be described to others – pre-prepare assertive 'I' statements so everyone is ready and doesn't slip into being aggressive or passive?

How will focus and optimism be maintained? How will problems be acknowledged but channelled into a positive outcome?

What tactics will be adopted to make sure that 'old' emotions in the situation do not take over and detract from the goal?

How will people 'take care of themselves' – it's hard to make personal changes when over-tired, over-wrought, under-nourished etc?

Decision 3 – do it (yes or no)?

STEP 4 – MONITOR THE EFFECTS

Capture thoughts and feelings, what happened and what can be learned from the experience:

What happened?
How do I or we feel now?
How do others feel now?
Was it worth it?

Decision 4 – would I do it differently next time (yes or no)?

CHAPTER 10

Final Thoughts and the Way Ahead

This book is based on the premise that there is a problem with risk management as currently understood and practised. Despite many years of development, with good agreement on the key principles and concepts, a proven toolkit with mature infrastructure support available, and a broad base of ongoing research, the areas where risk management is supposed to add value still continue to experience difficulty and failure. The reasons are many and various, but a common root is the effect of the human dimension in risk management. Too many risk practitioners (and the recipients of their services) act as if they believe that effective risk management simply requires attention to tools and techniques, systems and processes. They seem to forget that these are all operated by people, each of whom is a complex individual influenced by many different factors. This is further complicated by the fact that most risk management is undertaken by people working in groups, introducing additional layers of complexity through relationships and group dynamics.

In theory, implementation of risk management should be simple, whether it be strategic (mission, corporate governance, reputation and so on), tactical (bid, project, programme and so on), or operational (safety, security, business continuity and so on). There are many standards and guidelines defining current best practice for risk management in these different settings, and there is wide agreement on the required components of an effective risk management process. Standards are supported by books, journals and training courses explaining how to do it in practice. Professional bodies offer qualifications to certify capability, and consultancies provide expert input for specialized applications.

SIMPLE BUT DIFFICULT

With this wealth of resources, why then does risk management so often fail to deliver the promised benefits? One key is the recognition that just because something is *simple* does not mean that it is *easy*. It is simple to state that risk exists and can be identified (defined as uncertainties that if they occur would matter since they would have a positive or negative effect on achievement of objectives). It is also simple to say that risk should be managed proactively. The risk management process can be simply explained (define objectives; identify risks; assess their significance; determine appropriate responses; implement responses and monitor their effect; feedback, review and update). Most of the common risk techniques are simply structured common sense (though it is true that common sense is not very common), and are simple to understand.

If it is all so simple, there must be some other reason to explain why risk management is not working as expected. If simple is not the same as easy, what is it that makes the various simple components of risk management hard to implement?

The earlier discussion identified a wide range of Critical Success Factors (CSFs) for effective risk management (see Table 2.1), each of which is required if risk management is to succeed. But CSF might also stand for 'Critical Source of Failure', since the absence of these factors will ensure that risk management is unable to deliver the promised benefits. Most agree that the influence of people on the risk process is the most significant CSF, in both senses of the phrase, since people can either make or break the effectiveness of risk management. This is particularly true of the risk attitudes adopted by individuals and groups. Where the effect of risk attitude on risk management is understood and managed intelligently, it acts as a CSF and promotes risk management effectiveness. Conversely where risk attitudes are ignored or unmanaged, this becomes a Critical Source of Failure, leading to ineffective management of risk, with the inevitable adverse impact on achievement of objectives

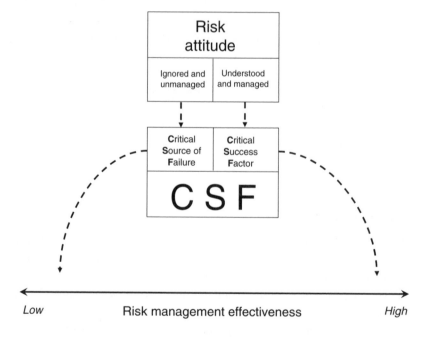

Figure 10.1   Risk attitude as a CSF for effective risk management

(see Figure 10.1). It is this central influence of people on the risk process that is largely responsible for making simple risk management hard to implement successfully and effectively.

Human factors influence risk management in a wide range of ways, and attention has increasingly been focused on these as a means of increasing risk management effectiveness. The term 'risk attitude' encapsulates much of the human factor domain, referring to the way in which individuals and groups choose to position themselves in relation to significant uncertainty. Consequently it can be argued that an ability to understand and manage risk attitudes would be a major step forward in improving the management of risk. And since risk attitudes exist at all levels in an organization, from the individual through working teams, departments, divisions, functional groups, management teams, the whole organization and even its cultural environment, understanding and managing risk attitudes can contribute to all levels of risk management.

Two key elements are required to enable this to be achieved:

- *understanding of risk attitudes* at all levels where they exist and matter;

- approaches which allow proactive *management of risk attitudes*.

DIFFICULTIES IN UNDERSTANDING RISK ATTITUDE

Earlier chapters in Part 2 have presented a coherent framework within which risk attitudes can be defined and understood, describing the risk attitude spectrum on which the chosen response of each individual or group can be placed in relation to any given uncertain event or situation. This represents a continuous range of attitudes, though it is useful to define some positional shorthand terms such as risk-averse, risk-tolerant, risk-neutral or risk-seeking. However, the use of these should not tempt people into thinking that each individual or group must fall into one of four well-defined camps. Reality is much more complex than that, adding to the 'simple but difficult' dimension.

A number of factors can be identified which complicate the understanding of risk attitudes, including the following:

- Risk attitudes are *situational*. Consequently neither individuals nor groups always display the same risk attitude under all circumstances. In some cases a person or group may be risk-averse, but the same person or group might be risk-tolerant in another situation. The risk attitudes adopted by individuals and groups are affected by *perceptual factors*, which influence the way in which uncertainty is perceived in a given situation. Although these factors and their effects can be described with some precision, they are often present in combination and interact with each other, making it harder to predict how they will influence risk attitude in practice.

- The position occupied on the risk attitude spectrum is influenced by the action of *heuristics*, of which there are a large number capable of affecting both individuals and groups. Like perceptual factors, each heuristic can be defined clearly in isolation, but in practice they operate together, complicating their influence on risk attitude. Some heuristics reinforce each other (for example cultural conformity and groupthink), where others have opposing effects (such as the Moses Factor and cautious shift). Further complexity arises through the interaction of heuristics with perceptual factors.

- The initial risk attitude displayed by an individual or a group is usually adopted *subconsciously*, though the precise mechanism by which this position is reached is not fully understood. Two competing theories exist (illustrated in Figures 9.2 and 9.3), differing in when the influence of perceptual factors and heuristics occurs. One possibility is that a particular individual or group always adopts the same default risk attitude, which is then modified by the effect of perception and heuristics. Alternatively the influencing factors might operate prior to the subconscious selection of risk attitude. In either case, the subconscious element of the process by which risk attitudes are adopted makes their diagnosis significantly more difficult.

- *Groups are comprised of individuals*, and although the risk attitudes of group members play a significant part in influencing the approach to risk adopted by the group as a whole, the effect of group dynamics at various levels complicates the situation. Each working team exists in a complex network of hierarchical and overlapping groups, with many interactions which are hard to define and harder to understand.

- Each risk attitude held by any individual or group is a *choice*, at least in theory, although the operation of strong and long-held habits can give the impression of involuntary adoption of a particular position. This means that the position on the risk attitude spectrum occupied by an individual or group can be varied consciously, depending on their level of emotional literacy. Since it is not possible for an outside observer to determine precisely how emotionally literate an individual or group may be, the extent to which choice is operational and freely exercised cannot be measured unambiguously.

These and other factors result in significant challenges for those wishing to *understand risk attitudes* as a precursor to their proactive management. Oversimplification is the enemy of understanding, though it is a common strategy, and the danger is that thinking becomes simplistic. As Albert Einstein (1879–1955) said, 'Everything should be made as simple as possible, but not simpler.' And his close contemporary, the American author and humorist Henry Louis Mencken (1880–1956) is quoted as saying 'For every complex problem, there is a solution that is simple, neat and wrong.'

DIFFICULTIES IN MANAGING RISK ATTITUDE

If understanding risk attitude is difficult, then its management is more so. Although human factors are often referred to as 'soft', dealing with them in practice can be 'hard'. This is not only because understanding must precede management, and any difficulties in the understanding element will be inherited when it comes to management. There are also features inherent in the management process itself which are necessarily complex, and which cannot be simplified without losing effectiveness.

It might appear straightforward to say that having identified the current risk attitude of an individual or group, all that is needed is to determine whether this is appropriate, and change it if required. While this statement is simple, each of its three component parts is significantly complex to implement:

- *Identify current risk attitude.* There are no reliable or precise diagnostic indicators of risk attitude currently available. It is therefore not possible to define unambiguously either the starting point for the change, or the desired end-point. Simple instruments exist which can divide people or groups into the four main headline categories of risk-averse/risk-tolerant/risk-neutral/risk-seeking, but this may not give the required degree of granularity to support change. For example in one case it may simply be necessary to move from risk-seeking to risk-averse, and the use of these generic labels may be sufficient. However, the situation is different if the required change is from strongly risk-tolerant to slightly risk-seeking, and without high-granularity diagnostic tools such terms cannot be interpreted objectively.

- *Determine whether current risk attitude is appropriate.* It is not clear how to determine unambiguously what risk attitude might be appropriate for a given situation. The key element to be considered is the effect on achievement of objectives, as emphasized by the key definitions of risk ('any uncertainty that if it occurred would affect achievement of one or more objectives'), and attitude ('chosen state of mind or disposition in relation to a given objective'). In both cases the main element to be considered is the potential for affecting objectives, leading to a working definition of risk attitude as 'a chosen response to uncertainty that matters, driven by perception'. Despite these clear definitions, it is not always immediately clear how selection of different risk attitudes would in fact affect achievement of objectives. For example where a trouble-shooting interim manager has been brought in to rescue an ailing department, is it more appropriate to be risk-averse and seek to remove uncertainty from the situation, or is a risk-seeking approach required to tackle the crisis and bring radical change?

- *Change risk attitude if required.* The change process involves a significant degree of investment and commitment. The previous chapter outlined a process for applying the concepts of emotional literacy to identification and modification of risk attitude (Figure 9.5 and Table 9.1), which can be applied to both individuals and groups. Though this process appears to be simple it is by no means easy. Each step in the process asks a number of subsidiary questions, and answering these is not trivial. A degree of objectivity and self-awareness is required, which may not come naturally to some individuals and groups. Indeed the use of a skilled facilitator to assist an individual or group through the process might be required (bearing in mind that 'facilitator' is derived from the Latin 'facilis' meaning easy – the role of the facilitator is to make the process easy for the participants).

It is therefore clear that a process for *managing risk attitude* may be simple to define and describe, but there are significant difficulties in its implementation.

TOO HARD?

It may never be possible to produce a consultant's model for understanding and managing risk attitude using applied emotional literacy. The complexities inherent in each dimension of the problem militate against developing a generic approach which can be applied off-the-shelf by following a predetermined process. Given that the challenge to understand and manage risk attitude is simple but difficult, the question arises of whether it is worth the effort. Would it not be better to stick to those elements of risk management which are well defined and proven? Why not invest in improving the tools and techniques, systems and processes, instead of worrying about the soft side of risk attitudes which seems so hard to grasp and even harder to modify?

The answer is two-fold. Firstly, incremental improvements in the mechanics of managing risk will never deliver the level of effectiveness required to match the relentless and increasing uncertainty facing every individual and organization. Formal approaches to risk management have been in existence for many years, yet the shortfall between promise and delivery remains. It is doubtful whether any radical improvement in risk management effectiveness can be achieved by simply doing the same thing but better. Quoting Einstein again, 'It is not possible to solve a problem using the same thinking that created it.' If effort is solely devoted to developing new tools and techniques, improving the system or streamlining the process, it is likely to produce only marginal increases in effective management of risk. Instead, attention must be paid to identifying and implementing those CSFs whose presence promote effective risk management (Critical Success Factors), and whose absence lead to failure (Critical Sources of Failure) – chief among which is the need to address the human element of risk management.

Secondly, the benefits available from proactive management of risk attitudes are so significant that they cannot be ignored. These include :

- ability to focus on objectives instead of being distracted or diverted by unmanaged personal issues;

- identification and removal of barriers to group performance posed by intrapersonal or interpersonal issues;

- improved motivation, both for individuals and for groups;

- more effective teamwork, understanding and building on the strengths of each member;

- increased individual and group health and wellbeing, through integration of chosen attitudes with core values and external requirements;

- reduction of stress which would otherwise arise from discord within individuals or teams, whether expressed or hidden;

- more effective leadership;

- ability to learn, both individual (personal development) and corporate (the learning organization).

These and other benefits are available only if the realities of the risk attitude challenge are recognized and tackled. The search for emotional literacy for individuals and groups is not an ethereal exercise in navel-gazing or self-discovery; instead it offers hard benefits to individuals and groups in terms of optimized performance and achievement of objectives. Although the process of understanding and managing risk attitudes through development of emotional literacy is not simple, it is worth doing, not only for the benefits available to the group or organization, but also for its contribution to the wellbeing and health of the individual.

FUTURE DEVELOPMENTS

In many ways the approach outlined in this book to understanding and managing risk attitude breaks new ground; yet the component parts already existed. Researchers and practitioners have for years known about the importance of risk attitudes, and have sought to understand them so that they can be managed. Similarly the field of emotional intelligence is not new, having its roots in ancient wisdom, though it has enjoyed a recent resurgence of interest. What is new is the recognition that emotional literacy is an essential prerequisite to both understanding and managing risk attitudes. Applying the insights of emotional literacy to the challenge of risk psychology offers a wealth of new avenues to explore, in both theory and practice. While the separate elements of risk psychology and emotional intelligence have existed for some time, each with its own industry and infrastructure, the synergistic approach described here of using applied emotional literacy to understand and manage risk attitudes is innovative.

There is, however, a number of areas where further development is needed if this approach is to be fully effective, and for it to be widely adopted into the business community. Following the steps presented in Chapter 9 will give individuals and groups a good start in being able to understand how they initially respond to significant uncertainty, whether this is appropriate, and how to change their current risk attitude if this is both necessary and desirable. Figure 9.5 and Table 9.1 outline a generic process for achieving this, which can be applied by any individual or group wishing to address risk attitudes proactively. But the complexities of the situation, in terms of both risk and emotion, require further work to develop a more robust approach which can be applied in all circumstances. Areas for future development might include the following:

- *Risk attitude diagnostic tools.* In order to answer the questions about what risk attitude is currently in place and what risk attitude might be appropriate for the situation, it is necessary to be able to diagnose risk attitude with some degree of accuracy. Current tools are quite crude, and most are only able to distinguish between the four main headline attitudes of risk-averse/risk-tolerant/risk-neutral/risk-seeking, but models are required to provide a more precise diagnostic framework on which detailed change can be built. Research is currently underway in several academic institutions, but a widely available diagnostic framework for risk attitude seems some way off.

- *Emotional literacy diagnostic tools.* Similarly, while there are several well-accepted frameworks for assessing emotional intelligence against different underlying models (see Appendix), those currently available lack the necessary diagnostic precision to be useful in assisting people to apply the approach to risk attitudes. It would be helpful for individuals and groups to be able to assess their degree of emotional literacy as an indicator of how successfully they might manage their risk attitudes, to benchmark their current emotional literacy and to measure improvement.

- *Robust generic models of risk attitude.* This area of risk psychology is still quite soft, with competing theories, developing concepts and emerging understanding. Development of the underlying theoretical framework would be useful, to provide a consensual foundation on which practitioners can build.

- *Specific instantiations of the generic model.* When agreement has been reached on a framework to represent risk attitude in general terms, it will be necessary to obtain data on how this applies specifically in different settings, for example job roles, industry types, or cultural variants. These specific applications can then act as a normative benchmark against which individuals, groups and organizations can assess their current position and determine what might be appropriate in given circumstances.

- *Case studies.* As with most emerging disciplines, progress will be made in this area through both theoretical advances and practical experiences. Much can be learned through recording, sharing and analysing instances where individuals, groups and organizations have attempted to use applied emotional literacy to understand and manage risk attitudes. Both success and failure stories will provide data to refine and improve the approach, and early-adopter individuals and organizations should be encouraged to share their experiences, both good and bad.

- *Managing group risk attitude.* The process for an individual person to manage their risk attitude in a particular situation is understood and described in this book. Managing group risk attitude is more difficult as would be expected given the added complexities when a number of different people work together. Although insights have been provided into understanding group risk attitude in this book, *managing* the multiple causes of bias on group risk attitude and decision-making is more difficult. Further work is needed to research the primary factors that influence group risk attitude. With this understanding it may be possible to provide guidance to decision-making groups to help them be aware of and compensate for those causes of bias that take them away from making appropriate decisions in uncertain situations.

CONCLUSION

Risk matters. Human factors matter. Risk attitudes matter. Emotions matter.

Each of these statements is connected by a focus on achievement of objectives, which are the measure of 'mattering'. The various dimensions of risk, human factors, risk attitude and emotions can each be described and assessed in isolation using well-proven models and frameworks. But they interact in powerful ways, and those interactions play a significant part in determining the effectiveness of each separate part. For individuals, groups and organizations who need to ensure that management of risk is effective, it is essential that they understand and manage all elements of this complex web. What part do human factors play in the risk management process? How are risk attitudes adopted and modified? How does the perception of risk affect behaviour and decision-making? Why are emotions important in the workplace?

Despite the complexities of this challenge, some core concepts have been defined and clarified in the preceding chapters. The broad outlines of a solution have been laid out, together with some suggestions for how the details might be filled in. For those pioneers wishing to take a lead in understanding and managing risk attitudes using applied emotional literacy, the insights presented here provide sufficient detail for them to begin. Applying the proven techniques discussed in these pages will start to unveil the mysteries of risk attitudes and allow steps to be taken towards improved risk management effectiveness.

Unmanaged risk attitudes pose a significant threat to the ability of individuals and groups to achieve their objectives. Developing emotional literacy at both individual and group levels offers a route towards understanding and managing risk attitudes, allowing the undoubted benefits to be reaped and creating a framework for ongoing learning and increased risk management effectiveness.

Emotional Intelligence/ Literacy Tools

A wide range of diagnostic tools is available for individuals to use to help them self-assess, and gain feedback from others, about the presence or absence of a range of dimensions of emotional intelligence/literacy. This is a mature market and the diagnostic tools available are solidly researched.

Products to assess risk attitudes are currently not available at the same degree of maturity, though work is underway in this area.

Since developing emotional literacy is an important aspect of understanding and managing risk attitudes, it is important to be aware of the main diagnostic tools in the area of emotional literacy.

Inclusion or omission of a tool in this appendix does not imply the existence or absence of endorsement, promotion or recommendation by the authors.

All the diagnostic tools are questionnaire based and designed for self-assessment by an individual as a minimum, and ideally for use on a 360° basis by the individual's manager(s), subordinate(s) and a number of peers.

All information presented about diagnostic tools was current at the time of writing. The relevant company names and web addresses should be consulted for up-to-date versions.

EMOTIONAL INTELLIGENCE INDIVIDUAL DIAGNOSTIC QUESTIONNAIRE

CENTRE FOR APPLIED EMOTIONAL INTELLIGENCE

www.appliedei.co.uk

166 questions answered using a 5-point scale

Scale 1: Self-regard

Scale 2: Regard for others

Scale 3: Self-awareness

Scale 4: Awareness of others

Scale 5: Emotional resilience

Scale 6: Personal power

Scale 7: Goal directedness

Scale 8: Flexibility

Scale 9: Personal openness

Scale 10: Trustworthiness

Scale 11: Trust

Scale 12: Balanced outlook

Scale 13: Emotional expression and control

Scale 14: Conflict handling

Scale 15: Interdependence

Scale 16: Accurate self-assessment

EMOTIONAL COMPETENCY INVENTORY

HAY ACQUISITION COMPANY INTERNATIONAL INC.

www.haygroup.com

110 questions answered using an 8-point scale

Personal Competences – determine how we manage ourselves
Self-awareness
  Emotional awareness
  Accurate self-assessment
  Self-confidence
Self-management
  Self-control
  Trustworthiness
  Conscientiousness
  Adaptability
  Achievement orientation
  Initiative

Social Competences – determine how we handle relationships
Social awareness
  Empathy
  Organizational awareness
  Service orientation
Social skills
  Developing others
  Leadership
  Influence
  Communication
  Change catalyst
  Conflict management
  Building bonds
  Teamwork and collaboration

BarOn Emotional Quotient Inventory® (BarOn EQ-I)

MHS EMOTIONAL INTELLIGENCE

www.emotionalintelligencemhs.com

133 questions answered using a 5-point scale

Intrapersonal scales

Self-regard

Emotional self-awareness

Assertiveness

Independence

Self-actualization

Interpersonal scales

Empathy

Social responsibility

Interpersonal relationship

Adaptability scales

Reality testing

Flexibility

Problem-solving

Stress management scale

Stress tolerance

Impulse control

General mood scales

Optimism

Happiness

EQ Map™ Questionnaire

Q-METRICS

www.qmetricseq.com

262 questions answered using a 5-point scale

Section 1: Current environment
 Scale 1: Life events
 Scale 2: Work pressures
 Scale 3: Personal pressures

Section II: Emotional literacy
 Scale 4: Emotional self-awareness
 Scale 5: Emotional expression
 Scale 6: Emotional awareness of others

Section III: EQ competencies
 Scale 7: Intentionality
 Scale 8: Creativity
 Scale 9: Resilience
 Scale 10: Interpersonal connections
 Scale 11: Constructive discontent

Section IV: EQ values and beliefs
 Scale 12: Compassion
 Scale 13: Outlook
 Scale 14: Intuition
 Scale 15: Trust radius
 Scale 16: Personal power
 Scale 17: Integrity

Section V: EQ outcomes
 Scale 18: General health
 Scale 19: Quality of life
 Scale 20: Relationship quotient
 Scale 21: Optimal performance

Emotional SMARTS™ Questionnaire

DONALDSON & ASSOCIATES, INC.

www.emotionalsmarts.com

94 questions answered using a 4-point scale

Awareness skills
  Emotional self-awareness
  Emotional management
  Assertiveness
  Goal achievement
  Optimism

Behavioural skills
  Independence
  Stress management
  Impulse control
  Conflict management

Contact skills
  Relationship building
  Empathy
  Social responsibility

Decision-making skills
  Problem identification
  Creativity
  Selecting solutions
  Reality testing

Bibliography and Further Reading

Adams, J. 1995. *Risk: The Policy Implications of Risk Compensation and Plural Rationalities*. UCL Press: London, UK. ISBN 1-857-28067-9.

Adams, J. 1999. *Risky Business*. Adam Smith Institute: London, UK. ISBN 1-902-73706-7.

Andersen, E. S. 2003. 'Understanding your project organisation's character'. *Project Management J*. **34** (4), pp. 4–11.

Association for Project Management. 2004. *Project Risk Analysis & Management (PRAM) Guide (second edition)*. APM Publishing: High Wycombe, Bucks, UK. ISBN 1-903494-12-5.

Association for Project Management. 2006. *APM Body of Knowledge* (fifth edition). Association for Project Management: High Wycombe, Bucks, UK. ISBN 1-903494-13-3.

Australian/New Zealand Standard AS/NZS 4360:2004. *Risk Management*. Standards Australia, Homebush NSW 2140, Australia, and Standards New Zealand, Wellington 6001, New Zealand. ISBN 0-7337-5904-1.

Baldwin, D. G. 2001. 'How to win the blame game'. *Harvard Business Review*. **79** (7), pp. 55–62.

Bandler, R. & Grinder, J. 1979. *Frogs into Princes*. Real People Press. ISBN 0-911-22619-2.

Bannister, J. 2001. 'Risk paranoia'. *InfoRM, journal of the UK Institute of Risk Management*, January/February 2001, pp. 12–14.

Barnett, J. & Breakwell, G. M. 2001. 'Risk perception and experience: hazard personality profiles and individual differences'. *Risk Analysis*. **21** (1), pp. 171–177.

Barsade, S. 2000. *The Ripple Effect: Emotional Contagion in Groups*. Working paper 98, Yale School of Management: New Haven, Connecticut.

Bartels, A. & Zeki, S. 2000. 'The neural basis of romantic love'. *NeuroReport*. **17** (11), pp. 3829–3834.

Bartels, A. & Zeki, S. 2004. 'The neural correlates of maternal and romantic love'. *NeuroImage*. **21** (3), pp. 1155–1166.

Bartlett, J. 2002. *Managing Risk for Projects and Programmes: A Risk Handbook*. Project Manager Today Publications: Hook, Hampshire, UK. ISBN 1-900391-10-4.

Bazerman, M. 1998. *Judgment in Managerial Decision-making (fourth edition)*. Wiley: Chichester, UK. ISBN 0-471-17807-1.

Beattie, J., Baron, J., Hershey, J. C. & Spranca, M. D. 1994. 'Psychological determinants of decision attitude'. *J Behavioural Decision Making*. **7**, pp. 129–144.

Bennis, W. & Nanus, B. 1985. *Leaders: Strategies for Taking Charge.* Harper and Row: New York. ISBN 0-060-15246-X.

Berne, E. 1961. *Transactional Analysis in Psychotherapy.* Ballantine Books (reissued 1986). ISBN 0-345-33836-7.

Bernstein, P. L. 1996. *Against the Gods – the Remarkable Story of Risk.* Wiley, Chichester, UK. ISBN 0-471-12104-5.

Borge, D. 2001. *The Book of Risk.* Wiley: Chichester, UK. ISBN 0-471-32378-0.

Bown, N. J., Read, D. & Summers, B. 2003. 'The lure of choice'. *J Behavioural Decision Making.* **16**, pp. 297–308.

British Standard BS6079-3:2000. *Project Management – Part 3: Guide to the Management of Business-related Project Risk.* British Standards Institute: London, UK. ISBN 0-580-33122-9.

Brown, A. 1995. *Organisational Culture.* Pitman Publishing: London, UK. Second edition (1998). ISBN 0-273-63147-0.

BS IEC 62198:2001. *Project Risk Management – Application Guidelines.* British Standards Institute: London, UK. ISBN 0-580-39019-5.

BSI PD 6668:2000. *Managing Risk for Corporate Governance.* British Standards Institute: London, UK. ISBN 0580-33246-2.

BSI PD ISO/IEC Guide 73:2002. *Risk Management – Vocabulary – Guidelines for Use in Standards.* British Standards Institute: London, UK. ISBN 0-580-40178-2.

Bukszar, E. & Connolly, T. 1998. 'Hindsight bias and strategic choice: Some problems in learning from experience'. *Academy of Management Journal.* **31** (3), pp. 628–641.

Burgess, M. 1999. *Living Dangerously: The Complex Science of Risk.* Channel 4 Television: London ,UK. ISBN 1-85144-252-9.

Cabanis-Brown, J. 1999. 'The human task of a project leader: Daniel Goleman on the value of high EQ'. *PM Network.* **13** (11), pp. 38–41.

Carroll, J. S. 1978. 'The effect of imagining an event on expectations for the event: An interpretation in terms of availability heuristic'. *J Experimental Psychology.* **17**, pp. 88–96.

Cartwright, D. & Zander, A. (eds). 1968. *Group Dynamics: Research and theory.* Harper & Row: New York, US. ISBN 0-060-41201-1.

Casper, C. M. 2002. 'Using Emotional Intelligence to improve project performance'. Proceedings of the 33rd Annual Project Management Institute Seminars & Symposium (PMI 2002), presented in San Antonio, US, 7–8 October 2002.

Chapman, C. B. & Ward, S. C. 1997. *Project Risk Management: Processes, techniques and insights.* Wiley: Chichester, UK. ISBN 0-471-95804-2.

Chapman, C. B. & Ward, S. C. 2000. 'Estimation and evaluation of uncertainty – a minimalist first-pass approach'. *Int J Project Management.* **18** (6), pp. 369–383.

Chapman, C. B. & Ward, S. C. 2002. *Managing Project Risk and Uncertainty.* Wiley: Chichester, UK. ISBN 0-470-84790-5.

Charette, R. N. & Edrich, C. 2001. *Implementing Risk Management Best Practices.* Cutter Information Corp: Arlington MA, US.

Cherniss, C. & Goleman, D. (eds) 2001. *The Emotionally Intelligent Workplace.* Jossey-Bass: San Francisco, US. ISBN 0-7879-5690-2.

Cooper, D. 1997. 'Evidence from safety culture that risk perception is culturally determined'. *Int J Project & Business Risk Management.* **1** (2), pp. 185–202.

Cooper, D. F., Grey, S. J., Raymond, G. & Walker, P. 2004. *Project Risk Management Guidelines: Managing risk in large projects and complex procurements.* J. Wiley: Chichester, UK. ISBN 0-470-02281-7.

Cooper, R. K. & Sawaf, A. 1997. *Executive EQ: Applying emotional intelligence in leadership and organisations.* The Berkley Publishing Group: US. ISBN 0-399-14294-0.

Cooper, R. K. 1997. 'Applying emotional intelligence in the workplace'. *Training and Development.* **51** (12), pp. 31–38.

Courtney, H., Kirkland, J. & Vignerie, P. 1997. 'Strategy under uncertainty'. *Harvard Business Review.* **75** (6), pp. 66–79.

Covey, S. R. 1990. *Seven Habits of Highly Effective People.* Free Press. ISBN 0-671-70863-5.

Davies, D. 2003. 'What crisis?' *Strategic Risk.* October 2003, pp. 28–32.

Davis, J. P. & Hall, J. W. 1998. 'Assembling uncertain evidence for decision making'. Proceedings of the third international conference on hydroinformatics (*Hydroinformatics 98*), pp. 1089–1094. Edited by Babovic, V. & Larsen, L. C. Balkema: Rotterdam, Netherlands. ISBN 90-5410-983-1.

de Bakker, K. 2003. 'Project risk management in cultural context'. Proceedings of 6th Annual Risk Conference, presented in London, UK, 28 November 2003.

de Cano, A. & de la Cruz, M. P. 1998. 'The past, present and future of project risk management'. *Int J Project & Business Risk Management.* **2** (4), pp. 361–387.

Deal, T. E. & Kenned, A. A. 1982. *Corporate Cultures: The rites and rituals of corporate life.* Addison-Wesley: Reading MA, US. ISBN 0-021-10277-3.

Dembo, R. S. & Freeman, A. 1998. *Seeing Tomorrow – Rewriting the rules of risk.* Wiley. ISBN 0-471-24736-7.

Descartes, R. 1990. *Les passions de l'âme.* Hackett Publishing Company: US. ISBN 0-872-20036-1.

Dorofee, A. J. et al. 1996. *Continuous Risk Management Guidebook.* SEI Carnegie Mellon University.

Druskat, V. U. & Wolff, S. B. 2001. 'Building the emotional intelligence of groups'. *Harvard Business Review.* **79** (3), pp. 80–90.

Dulewicz, V. & Higgs, M. 1998. *Emotional Intelligence: Managerial fad or valid construct (Henley Working Paper).* Henley Management College: Henley, UK. ISBN 1-861-81076-8.

Dulewicz, V. & Higgs, M. 1999. *Can Emotional Intelligence be Measured and Developed? (Henley Working Paper).* Henley Management College: Henley, UK. ISBN 1-861-81087-3.

Fahey, L. & Narayanan, V. K. 1986. *Macro-environmental Analyses for Strategic Management.* West Publishing. ISBN 0-314-85233-6.

Finucane, M. L., Alhakami, A., Slovic, P. & Johnson, S. M. 2000. 'The affect heuristic in judgements of risks and benefits'. *J Behavioural Decision Making*. **13**, pp. 1–17.

Fischhoff, B. 1985. 'Managing risk perceptions'. *Issues in Science and Technology*. **2** (1), pp. 83–96.

Fischhoff, B., Lichtenstein, S., Slovic, P., Derby, S. L. & Keeney, R. L. 1981. *Acceptable Risk*. Cambridge University Press: Cambridge, UK. ISBN 0-521-24164-2.

Flyvbjerg, B., Bruzelius, N. & Rothengatter, W. 2003. *Megaprojects and Risk: An anatomy of ambition*. Cambridge University Press: Cambridge, UK. ISBN 0-521-80420-5.

Franklin, J. (ed). 1998. *The Politics of Risk Society*. Polity Press: Cambridge, UK. ISBN 0-745-61924-X.

Frost, R. & Lathem, E. C. 2001. *The Poetry of Robert Frost*. Vintage. ISBN 0-099-42829-6.

Furedi, F. 2002. *The Culture of Fear: Risk taking and the morality of low expectation (revised edition)*. Continuum International Publishing Group. ISBN 0-826-45930-7.

Gardner, H. 1993. *Frames of Mind: The theory of multiple intelligences (tenth anniversary edition)*. Basic Books: New York, US. ISBN 0-465-02510-2.

Gardner, H. 1993. *Multiple Intelligences: The theory in practice*. Basic Books: New York, US. ISBN 0-465-01822-X.

Gardner, H. 2000. *Intelligence Reframed: Multiple intelligences for the 21st century*. Basic Books: New York, US. ISBN 0-465-02611-7.

Garvin, D. A. & Roberts, M. A. 2001. 'What you don't know about making decisions'. *Harvard Business Review*. **79** (8), pp. 108–116.

Gilovich, T. Griffin, D. & Kahneman, D. (eds). 2002. *Heuristics and Biases: The psychology of intuitive judgement*. Cambridge University Press: Cambridge, UK. ISBN 0-521-79679-2.

Goleman, D. 1995. *Emotional Intelligence: Why it can matter more than IQ*. Bloomsbury Publishing plc: London, UK. ISBN 0-7475-2830-6.

Goleman, D. 1998. 'What makes a leader?' *Harvard Business Review*. **76** (6), pp. 93–104.

Goleman, D. 1998. *Working with Emotional Intelligence*. Bloomsbury Publishing plc: London, UK. ISBN 0-7475-3984-7.

Goleman, D. 2001. *Emotionally Intelligent Workplace: How to select for, measure and improve emotional intelligence in individuals, groups and organizations*. Jossey-Bass: Hackensack, NJ, US. ISBN 0-787-95690-2.

Goleman, D. 2003. *Destructive Emotions*. Bloomsbury Publishing plc: London, UK. ISBN 0-7475-5393-9.

Goleman, D., Boyatzis, R. & McKee, A. 2001. 'Primal leadership: The hidden driver of great performance'. *Harvard Business Review*. December 2001, pp. 42–51.

Goleman, D., Boyatzis, R. & McKee, A. 2004. *Primal Leadership: Learning to Lead with Emotional Intelligence*. Harvard Business School Press. ISBN 1-591-39184-9.

Greenwood, M. 1998. 'Measuring risk behaviour: An introduction to the risk behaviour profiler'. *Int J Project & Business Risk Mgt*. **2** (3), pp. 273–288.

Grey, S. 1995. *Practical Risk Assessment for Project Management.* Wiley: Chichester, UK. ISBN 0-471-93978-X.

Hall, E. & Hall, M. 1990. *Understanding Cultural Differences.* Intercultural Press: Yarmouth, US. ISBN 1-877-86407-2.

Hall, E. M. 1998. *Managing Risk – Methods for software systems development.* Addison Wesley Longman: Reading MA, US. ISBN 0-201-25592-8.

Hall, E. M. 1999. 'Risk management Return On Investment'. *Systems Engineering.* 2 (3), pp. 177–180.

Hammond, J. S., Keeney, R. L. & Raiffa, H. 1998. 'The hidden traps in decision making'. *Harvard Business Review.* September/October 1998, pp. 47–58.

Harris, A. & Harris, T. 1985. *Staying OK.* Arrow Books in 1995. ISBN 0-09-955251-5.

Harris, T. 1970. *I'm OK – You're OK* (formerly published as *The Book of Choice*). Pan Books Ltd: UK. ISBN 0-330-23543-5.

Harrison, R. 1972. 'Understanding your organisation's character'. *Harvard Business Review.* 50 (3), pp. 119–128.

Higgs, M. & Dulewicz, V. 2002. *Can Emotional Intelligence be Developed?* (Henley Working Paper). Henley Management College: Henley, UK. ISBN 1-861-81128-4.

Higgs, M. & Dulewicz, V. 2002. *Making Sense of Emotional Intelligence (second edition).* Nelson: UK. ISBN 0-708-70367-4.

Higgs, M. & McGuire, V. 2001. *Emotional Intelligence and Culture: An Exploration of the Relationship Between Individual Emotional Intelligence and Organisational Culture* (Henley Working Paper). Henley Management College: Henley, UK. ISBN 1-861-81107-1.

Hillson, D. A. 2000. 'Project risk management – where next?' *The Project Management Yearbook 2000*, pp. 55–59. Association for Project Management (APM): High Wycombe, Bucks, UK. ISBN 1-869865-99-5.

Hillson, D. A. 2002. 'Critical success factors for effective risk management'. *PM Review* (four-part series), July–December 2002.

Hillson, D. A. 2002. 'Extending the risk process to manage opportunities'. *Int J Project Management,* 20 (3), pp. 235–240.

Hillson, D. A. 2002. 'What is risk? Towards a common definition'. *InfoRM, Journal of the UK Institute of Risk Management.* April 2002, pp. 11–12.

Hillson, D. A. 2003. *Effective Opportunity Management for Projects: Exploiting positive risk.* Marcel Dekker: New York, US. ISBN 0-8247-4808-5.

Hillson, D. A. (ed) 2006. *The Risk Management Universe: A guided tour.* British Standards Institution: London, UK. ISBN 0-580-43777-9.

Hillson, D. A. & Murray-Webster, R. 2004. 'Understanding and managing risk attitude'. Proceedings of 7th Annual Risk Conference, held in London, UK, 26 November 2004.

Hillson, D. A. & Murray-Webster, R. 2005. 'Using emotional literacy to understand and manage risk attitude'. Proceedings of ESRC Social Contexts And Responses to

Risk (SCARR) Launch Conference, held in Canterbury, UK, 28–29 January 2005.

Hillson, D. A. & Murray-Webster, R. 2006. 'Managing risk attitude using emotional literacy'. *Proceedings of PMI Global Congress 2006*. EMEA, held in Madrid, Spain, 9 May 2006.

HM Government Cabinet Office Strategy Unit. 2002. *Risk: Improving government's capability to handle risk and uncertainty*. Report ref 254205/1102/D16, Crown copyright 2002.

Hofstede, G. H. 1982. *Culture's Consequences: International differences in work-related values* (abridged edition). Sage Publications Inc: Newbury Park, California, US. ISBN 0-8039-1306-0.

Hofstede, G. H. 2001. *Culture's Consequences: Comparing values, behaviours, institutions, and organisations across nations (second edition)*. Sage Publications Inc: Thousand Oaks, California, US. ISBN 0-8039-7324-1.

Hulett, D. T., Hillson, D. A. & Kohl, R. 2002. 'Defining Risk: A Debate'. *Cutter IT Journal*. **15** (2), pp. 4–10.

Institute of Chartered Accountants in England and Wales (ICAEW). 1998. *Financial Reporting of Risk: Proposals for a statement of business risk*. ICAEW: London, UK.

Institute of Chartered Accountants in England and Wales (ICAEW). 1999. *Internal Control: Guidance for directors on the Combined Code*. ICAEW: London, UK. ISBN 1-84152-010-1.

Institute of Chartered Accountants in England and Wales (ICAEW). 1999. *No Surprises: The case for better risk reporting*. ICAEW: London, UK.

Institute of Risk Management (IRM), National Forum for Risk Management in the Public Sector (ALARM), & Association of Insurance and Risk Managers (AIRMIC). 2002. *A Risk Management Standard*. IRM/ALARM/AIRMIC: London, UK.

Institution of Civil Engineers (ICE) and the Actuarial Professional. 2005. *Risk Analysis & Management for Projects (RAMP) (second edition)*. Thomas Telford. ISBN 0-7277-3390-7.

Jaafari, A. 2001. 'Management of risks, uncertainties and opportunities on projects: Time for a fundamental shift'. *Int J Project Management*, **19** (2), pp. 89–101.

Janis, I. & Mann, L. 1979. *Decision Making: A psychological analysis of conflict, choice and commitment*. Houghton Mifflin: Boston, US. ISBN 0-029-16190-8.

Janis, I. 1972. *Victims of Groupthink: Psychological study of foreign-policy decisions and fiascos*. Houghton Mifflin: Boston, US. ISBN 0-395-14044-7.

Janis, I. 1982. *Groupthink: Psychological studies of policy decisions and fiascos*. Houghton Mifflin: Boston, US. ISBN 0-395-31704-5.

Jarrett, E. L. 2000. 'The role of risk in business decision-making'. *Research Technology Management (Industrial Research Institute)*, pp. 44–46.

Kähkönen, K. 2001. 'Integration of risk and opportunity thinking in projects'. Proceedings of the 4th European Project Management Conference (PMI Europe 2001), presented in London, UK, 6–7 June 2001.

Kahn, B. E. & Sarin, R. K. 1988. 'Modelling ambiguity in decisions under uncertainty'. *J Consumer Research.* **15** (2), pp. 265–272.

Kahneman, D. & Tversky, A. 1979. 'Prospect theory: An analysis of decision under risk'. *Econometrica.* **47** (2), pp. 263–297.

Kahneman, D., Slovic, P. & Tversky, A. (eds). 1986. *Judgement under Uncertainty: Heuristics and biases.* Cambridge University Press: Cambridge, UK. ISBN 0-521-24064-6.

Kelly, P. 2002. 'Risk decisions under uncertainty'. *InfoRM, journal of the UK Institute of Risk Management.* October 2002, pp. 12–14.

Korzybski, A. 1995. *Science and Sanity: An introduction to non-Aristotelian systems and general semantics (fifth edition).* Institute of General Semantics. ISBN 0-937-29801-8.

Krimsky, S. & Golding, D. 1992. *Social Theories of Risk.* Praeger: Westport, CT, US. ISBN 0-275-94317-8.

Loewenstein, G. F., Weber, E. U., Hsee, C. K. & Welch, E. S. 2001. 'Risk as feelings'. *Psychological Bulletin.* **127** (2), pp. 267–286.

Lopes, L. L. 1987. 'Between hope and fear: The psychology of risk'. *Advances in Experimental Social Psychology.* **20**, pp. 255–295.

Luft, J. & Ingham, H. 1955. 'The Johari Window; A graphic model of interpersonal awareness'. Proceedings of the Western Training Laboratory in Group Development (Los Angeles: UCLA Extension Office).

Luft, J. 1961. 'The Johari Window', *Human Relations Training News.* **5** (1), pp. 6–7.

MacCrimmon, K. R. & Wehrung, D. A. 1988. *Taking Risks: The management of uncertainty.* Macmillan Press: US. ISBN 0-029-19563-2.

MacCrimmon, K. R. & Wehrung, D. A. 1990. 'Characteristics of risk-taking executives'. *Management Science.* **36** (4), pp. 422–435.

MacLean, P. D. 1974. *Triune Conception of the Brain and Behaviour.* University of Toronto Press. ISBN 0-802-03299-0.

MacLean, P. D. 1989. *The Triune Brain in Evolution: Role in palaeocerebral functions.* Kluwer Academic. ISBN 0-306-43168-8.

Marris, C. & Langford, I. 1996. 'No cause for alarm'. *New Scientist.* 28 September 1996, pp. 36–39.

Marsh, J. G. & Shapira, Z. 1987. 'Managerial perspectives on risk and risk-taking'. *Management Science.* **33** (11), pp. 1404–1418.

Mayer, J. D. & Geher, G. 1996. 'Emotional intelligence and the identification of emotion'. *Intelligence.* **22**, pp. 89–113.

Mayer, J. D. & Salovey, P. 1995. 'Emotional intelligence and the construction and regulation of feelings'. *Applied and Preventive Psychology.* **4**, pp. 197–208.

Mayer, J. D., DiPaolo, M. T. & Salovey, P. 1990. 'Perceiving affective content in ambiguous visual stimuli: A component of emotional intelligence'. *J Personality Assessment.* **54**, pp. 772–781.

McCray, G. E., Purvis, R. L. & McCray, C. G. 2002. 'Project management under uncertainty: The impact of heuristics and biases'. *Project Management Journal.* **33** (1), pp. 49–57.

McGowan, C. 2000. *Elements of Risk: Attitude measurement and the implications for senior management.* MBA research thesis, University of Otago: Dunedin, New Zealand.

McKenna, S. 2001. 'Organisational complexity and perceptions of risk. *Risk Management: An International Journal,* **3** (2), pp. 53–64.

Merlevede, P. E., Bridoux, D. & Vandamme, R. 2001. *Seven Steps to Emotional Intelligence.* Crown House Publishing Limited: UK. ISBN 1-899-83650-0.

Moorhead, G., Ference, R. & Neck, C. P. 1991. 'Group decision fiascos continue: Space shuttle Challenger and a revised groupthink framework'. *Human Relations.* **44** (6), pp. 539-550.

Mukherji, A. & Wright, P. 2002. 'Re-examining the relationship between action preferences and managerial risk behaviours'. *J Managerial Issues.* **4** (3), pp. 314–330.

National Standard of Canada CAN/CSA-Q850-97. *Risk Management: Guideline for decision-makers.* Canadian Standards Association: Ontario, Canada. ISSN 0317-5669.

Navare, J. 2003. 'Process or behaviour: Which is the risk and which is to be managed?'. *Managerial Finance.* **29** (5/6), pp. 6–9.

Newland, K. E. 1997. 'Benefits of project risk management to an organisation'. *Int J Project & Business Risk Mgt.* **1** (1), pp. 1–14.

Nordland, O. 1999. 'A discussion of risk tolerance principles'. *Safety Critical Systems Club Newsletter.* **8** (3), pp. 1–4.

Norem, J. K. 2002. *The Positive Power of Negative Thinking.* Basic Books: New York, US. ISBN 0-465-05139-1.

Oldfield, A. & Ocock, M. 1997. 'Managing project risks: the relevance of human factors'. *Int J Project & Business Risk Mgt.* **1** (2), pp. 99–109.

Oldfield, A. 1998. 'The human factor in risk management'. *Project.* **10** (10), pp. 13–15.

Osborne, A. F. 1963. *Applied Imagination: Principles and procedures of creative problem solving (third edition).* Charles Scribners: New York, US.

Palmer, C. G. S., Carlstrom, L. K. & Woodward, J. A. 2001. 'Risk perception and ethnicity'. *Risk, Decision & Policy.* **6** (3), pp. 187–206.

Pender, S. 2001. 'Managing incomplete knowledge: Why risk management is not sufficient'. *Int J Project Management.* **19** (2), pp. 79–87.

Peterson, C. 2001. 'Assessing risk attitude for improved visibility to project risk'. Proceedings of the 4th European Project Management Conference (PMI Europe 2001), presented in London, UK, 6–7 June 2001.

Plous, S. 1993. *Psychology of Judgement and Decision-making.* McGraw-Hill. ISBN 0-070-50477-6.

Pooley, C., Turnbull, J. & Adams, M. 2004. 'Changes in everyday mobility in England since the 1940s'. *Belgeo (The Belgian Journal of Geography).* Special issue on Human Mobility in Europe (in press).

Pooley, C., Turnbull, J. & Adams, M. 2005. *A Mobile Century?: changes in everyday mobility in Britain in the twentieth century.* Ashgate: Aldershot, UK. ISBN 0-754-64181-3.

Pooley, R. 2001. 'International project teams – Bridging the culture gap'. Proceedings of the Effective Project Management 2001 Conference, held in London, UK, 30–31 October 2001.

Popper, K. R. 2002. *The Logic of Scientific Discovery (fifteenth edition).* Routledge: London, UK. ISBN 0-415-27843-0.

Pritchard, C. 2001. *Risk Management: Concepts and guidance.* ESI International. ISBN 1-890-36701-X.

Project Management Institute. 2004. *A Guide to the Project Management Body of Knowledge (PMBoK®), Third Edition.* Project Management Institute: Philadelphia, US. ISBN 1-930-69949-2.

Ropeik, D. & Slovic, P. 2003. 'Risk communication: A neglected tool in protecting public health'. *Risk in Perspective (Harvard Centre for Risk Analysis).* **11** (2).

Russo, J. E. 1990. *Decision Traps.* Fireside: US. ISBN 0-671-72609-9.

Salovey, P. & Mayer, J. D. 1990. 'Emotional intelligence'. *Imagination, Cognition, and Personality.* **9**, pp. 185–211.

Salovey, P. & Sluyter D. J. 1997. *Emotional Development and Emotional Intelligence.* Basic Books: New York , US. ISBN 0-465-09587-9.

Salovey, P., Brackett, M. A. & Mayer, J. D. 2004. *Emotional Intelligence: Key readings on the Mayer and Salovey model.* National Professional Resources Inc. ISBN 1-887-94372-2.

Schein, E. H. 2004. *Organisational Culture and Leadership (third edition).* Jossey-Bass. ISBN 0-787-96845-5.

Schneider, S. L. & Shanteau, J. (eds). 2003. *Emerging Perspectives on Judgement and Decision Research.* Cambridge University Press: Cambridge, UK. ISBN 0-521-52718-X.

Schuyler, J. 2000. 'Capturing judgements about risks and uncertainties'. *PM Network.* **14** (7), pp. 43–47.

Schuyler, J. 2001. *Risk and Decision Analysis in Projects (second edition).* Project Management Institute: Philadelphia, US. ISBN 1-880410-28-1.

Sennara, M. & Hartman, F. 2002. 'Managing cultural risks on international projects'. Proceedings of the 33rd Annual Project Management Institute Seminars & Symposium (PMI 2002), presented in San Antonio, US, 7–8 October 2002.

Sharp, P. 2001. *Nurturing Emotional Literacy, A practical guide for teachers, parents and those in the caring professions.* David Fulton Publishers Ltd: London. ISBN 1-853-46678-6.

Shoham, A. & Fiegenbaum, A. 2002. 'Competitive determinants of organisational risk-taking attitude: The role of strategic reference points'. *Management Decision.* **40** (2), pp. 127–141.

Simons, R. 1999. 'How risky is your business?' *Harvard Business Review.* May–June 1999, pp. 85–94.

Sitkin, S. B. & Weingart, L. R. 1995. 'Determinants of risky decision-making behaviour: A test of the mediating role of risk perceptions and propensity'. *Academy of Management J.* **38** (6), pp. 1573–1592.

Slovic, P. 1987. 'Perception of risk'. *Science.* **236**, pp. 280–285.

Slovic, P. 2000. *Perception of Risk.* Earthscan Press: London, UK. ISBN 1-853-83528-5.

Slovic, P. 2005. 'Emotion and reason in learning about risk'. Proceedings of ESRC Social Contexts And Responses to Risk (SCARR) Launch Conference, held in Canterbury, UK, 28–29 January 2005.

Slovic, P., Finucane, M. L., Peters, E. & MacGregor, D. G. 2004. 'Risk as analysis and risk as feelings: Some thoughts about affect, reason, risk and rationality'. *Risk Analysis.* **24** (2), pp. 311–322.

Spony, G. 2003. 'The development of a work-value model assessing the cumulative impact of individual and cultural differences on managers' work-value systems'. *International Journal of Human Resource Management.* **14** (4), pp. 658–79.

Steiner, C. & Perry, P. 1997. *Achieving Emotional Literacy: A personal program to increase your emotional intelligence.* Hearst Books. ISBN 0-380-97591-2.

Steiner, C. & Perry, P. 2000. *Achieving Emotional Literacy (second edition).* Barnes & Noble. ISBN 0-747-54135-3.

Steiner, C. 2003. *Emotional Literacy: Intelligence with a heart.* Personhood Press: Fawnskin, California, US. ISBN 1-932-18102-4.

Stock, M., Copnell, T. & Wicks, C. 1999. *The Combined Code: A practical guide.* Gee Publishing: London, UK. ISBN 0-860-89661-8.

Sutton, R. I. 2001. 'The weird rules of creativity'. *Harvard Business Review,* **79** (8), pp. 94–103.

Tice, L. 1997. *Smart Talk for Achieving Your Potential.* Executive Excellence Publishing. ISBN 0-963-49176-8.

Trompenaars, F. 2003. *Did the Pedestrian Die?* Capstone Publishing Limited: Oxford, UK. ISBN 1-84112-436-2.

Trompenaars, F. 2004. *Managing Change Across Corporate Cultures.* Capstone Publishing Ltd., Oxford, UK. ISBN 1-84112-578-4.

Trompenaars, F. & Hampden-Turner ,C. 1998. *Riding the Waves of Culture (second edition).* McGraw-Hill. ISBN 0-7863-1125-8.

Tuckman, B. 1965. 'Developmental sequence in small groups'. *Psychological Bulletin,* **63**, pp. 384–399.

Tversky, A. & Kahneman, D. 1971. 'Belief in the law of small numbers'. *Psychological Bulletin,* **76**, pp. 105–110.

Tversky, A. & Kahneman, D. 1973. 'Availability: A heuristic for judging frequency and probability'. *Cognitive Psychology.* **5**, pp. 207-232.

Tversky, A. & Kahneman, D. 1974. 'Judgement under uncertainty: Heuristics and biases'. *Science.* **185**, pp. 1124–1131.

Tversky, A. & Kahneman, D. 1981. 'The framing of decisions and the psychology of choice'. *Science.* **211**, pp. 453–458.

Tversky, A. & Kahneman, D. 1992. 'Advances in prospect theory: Cumulative representation of uncertainty'. *J Risk and Uncertainty.* **5**, pp. 297–323.

UK Association for Project Management. 2000. *Project Management Body of Knowledge, Fourth Edition.* APM: High Wycombe, Bucks, UK. ISBN 1-9034.

UK Office of Government Commerce (OGC). 2002. *Management of Risk – Guidance for practitioners.* The Stationery Office: London, UK. ISBN 0-1133-0909-0.

Vose, D. 2000. *Risk Analysis – A quantitative guide (second edition).* Wiley: Chichester, UK. ISBN 0-471-99765-X.

Ward, S. C. & Chapman, C. B. 2003. 'Transforming project risk management into project uncertainty management'. *Int J Project Management.* **21** (2), pp. 97–105.

Ward, S. C. 1999. 'Requirements for an effective project risk management process'. *Project Management Journal.* **30** (3,) pp. 37–43.

Ward, S. C., Klein, J. H., Avison, D. E., Powell, P. L. & Keen, J. 1997. 'Flexibility and the management of uncertainty: A risk management perspective'. *Int J Project & Business Risk Management.* **1** (2), pp. 131–145.

Watkins, M. D. & Bazerman, M. H. 2003. 'Predictable surprises: the disasters you should have seen coming'. *Harvard Business Review.* **81** (3), pp. 72–80.

Weisinger, H. 2000. *Emotional Intelligence at Work (second edition).* Jossey-Bass. ISBN 0-787-95198-6.

Williams, S. & Narendran, S. 1999. 'Determinants of managerial risk: Exploring personality and cultural influences'. *J Social Psychology.* **139** (1), pp. 102–125.

Williams, T. M. 2002. *Modelling Complex Projects.* Wiley: Chichester, UK. ISBN 0-471-89945-3.

Yates, J. F. (ed). 1992. *Risk-taking Behaviour.* Wiley: Chichester, UK. ISBN 0-471-92250-1.

Index

Risk Doctor & Partners
Company Services
www.risk-doctor.com
tel. +44(0)7717 665222

Risk Doctor & Partners provides *specialist risk management consultancy and training* from Dr David Hillson and senior associates who offer a high-quality professional service to clients across the globe. David Hillson is recognized internationally as a leading thinker and expert practitioner in risk management, and he is a popular conference speaker and regular author on the topic. Risk Doctor & Partners embodies David's unique ethos, blending leading-edge thinking with practical application and providing access to the latest developments in risk management best practice. Full details of the business are at www.risk-doctor.com.

Risk Doctor & Partners also maintains a network of people interested in risk management who want to keep in touch with latest thinking and practice. Risk Doctor Network members receive regular email briefings on current issues in risk management. Previous briefings can be downloaded from the website and are available in English, French, German, Spanish and Chinese. Many of David's papers can also be downloaded from the website.

The services offered by Risk Doctor & Partners include :

- **Coaching and mentoring**, providing personal input and support to key individuals or small teams, aiming to share and transfer expertise.

- **Organizational benchmarking**, using proven maturity model frameworks to understand current risk management capability in terms of risk culture, processes, experience and application, then defining realistic and achievable improvement targets, and action plans to enhance capability.

- **Process review**, comparing your risk management approach against best practice and recommending practical improvements to meet the specific challenges faced by your business.

- **Risk review**, assessing the risk exposure of your bid, project, programme or strategy, identifying and prioritizing threats and opportunities, and developing effective responses to optimize project performance and achievement of objectives.

- **Risk training**, offering a range of learning experiences designed to raise awareness, create understanding and develop skills, targeting senior management, programme/project managers, project teams and risk practitioners.

Lucidus Consulting
Company Services
www.lucidusconsulting.com
tel. +44(0)207 060 2196

Lucidus Consulting provides services from Ruth Murray-Webster, Peter Simon and selected associates to assist in the proper application of project and programme management.True to the name Lucidus, the company aims to create value by *shedding light on managed change.* To achieve this aim, the Lucidus Consulting team does three things.

- First, we provide practical advice and assistance based on intuitive and concise analysis of current situations.

- Second, we enable individuals and teams to take charge of their own change agenda by providing targeted assessment and development of competency.

- Third, we are able to practice what we preach, by providing timely and valuable interim management support to clients.

In addition, we publish monthly *Lucid Thoughts* on our website and in the UK project management journal *Project Manager Today. Lucid Thoughts* are personal reflections on an aspect of project or programme management upon which we have a particular and sometimes controversial view. Feedback from *Lucid Thoughts* readers encourages networking and debate on some of the hot topics related to managed change in organizations.

As one of the managing partners within Lucidus Consulting, Ruth Murray-Webster brings her particular fascination with the impact of human beings on organizational change to the company. If people make projects work then understanding human behaviour when working to deliver unique objectives through a transient, multi-functional team of people within the constraints of time, cost and specification must be a priority. Risk attitudes, as explored in this book, form an important part of this story.

Full details of the business are at www.lucidusconsulting.com. The website also offers Ruth's papers for download as well as a full set of *Lucid Thoughts.*

Understanding and Managing Risk Attitude in action

David Hillson and Ruth Murray-Webster are pleased to offer readers and others a suite of interventions designed to implement the ideas presented in this book. These cover the two key requirements of *understanding* and *managing*, and address the needs of both individuals and teams. Each event can be run on an in-house basis for clients who wish to maximize the benefits to their staff and teams. Public events will also be scheduled from time to time (contact training@risk-attitude.com for full details).

The starting place for everyone interested in developing their ability to manage risk attitude is the one-day *Understanding Risk Attitude Workshop*. Facilitated by both David and Ruth, this workshop covers all the main themes and learning contained within the book in a practical and fun way. Designed for a maximum of 12 people to maximize interaction, the workshop requires no previous knowledge or experience of risk attitudes or emotional literacy. However, maximum value will be gained by people who have already read the book and who have thought about the concepts and principles.

For those who have completed the Understanding Risk Attitude Workshop there are two options for support with Managing Risk Attitude:

- For individuals, David and Ruth offer a *Personal Coaching Day* to provide one-to-one support as the person works through a process of understanding and managing their own risk attitude in respect of a particular uncertain situation.

- For groups with a common objective, David and Ruth offer a *Team Coaching Workshop* where the members of a group facing a particular uncertain situation can together work through the process of understanding and managing their group risk attitude.

For further details of these and other services, visit www.risk-attitude.com.

If you have found this book useful you may be interested in other titles from Gower

Advanced Project Management
4th Edition
F.R. Harrison and Dennis Lock
0 566 07822 8

Accelerating Business and IT Change
Alan Fowler and Dennis Lock
0 566 08604 2

Benefit Realisation Management
Gerald Bradley
0 566 08687 5

The Bid Manager's Handbook
David Nickson
0 566 08512 7

Contracting for Engineering and Construction Projects
5th Edition
Peter Marsh
0 566 08282 9

Failsafe IS Project Delivery
Andrew Holmes
0 566 08255 1

Gower Handbook of Programme Management
Geoff Reiss, Malcolm Anthony, John Chapman,
Geof Leigh, Adrian Pyne and Paul Rayner
0 566 08603 4

GOWER

Gower Handbook of Project Management
3rd Edition
edited by J. Rodney Turner and Stephen J. Simister
0 566 08138 5 (hbk) 0 566 08397 3 (CD-ROM)

Law for Project Managers
David Wright
0 566 08601 8

Project Delivery in Business as Usual Organizations
Tim Carroll
0 566 08629 8

Project Management
8th Edition
Dennis Lock
0 566 08551 8

The Project Manager's Guide to Handling Risk
Alan Webb
0 566 08571 2

The Relationship Manager
Tony Davis and Richard Pharro
0 566 08463 5

Using Earned Value
Alan Webb
0 566 08533 X

For further information on these and all our titles visit
our website – **www.gowerpub.com**
All online orders receive a discount

GOWER